Cyber Security Risk Management Handbook: Fortify, Protect, Defend

Dravenius Queltharan

CYBER SECURITY RISK MANAGEMENT HANDBOOK: FORTIFY, PROTECT, DEFEND

First edition. August 21, 2025.

ISBN: 979-8231156238

Written by Dravenius Queltharan.

"Why I Stopped Sleeping and Started Risk Managing"

So, picture this: I'm sipping on lukewarm coffee at 2 a.m., staring at my laptop like it just confessed to cheating on me. An alert flashes across the screen. Another alert. Then fifteen more. I'm not in an action movie, but my heart is racing like I'm diffusing a digital bomb. A ransomware attack had just made itself very comfortable in the heart of our company's infrastructure, like a drunk guest who crashed the party, ate all the snacks, and set fire to the couch.

That was the moment I realized—risk management isn't just a checklist you awkwardly copy-paste from a PowerPoint deck. It's the only thing standing between your calm morning coffee and a full-blown, code-red meltdown with crying interns and lawyers huddled in a panic room. And I thought to myself: "You know what the world needs? A book about cyber risk management that doesn't make you want to shove your head into a firewall."

And thus, this book was born. Welcome to Cyber Security Risk Management Handbook: Fortify, Protect, Defend—your unofficial (but very practical) guide to not freaking out when the cyber demons come knocking.

Now, I know what you're thinking: "Another tech guy writing a book about risk. Wow. Riveting." But stay with me. Because this isn't your typical dry, corporate snooze-fest filled with acronyms that make your eyes glaze over like a donut. I mean, sure, we'll have acronyms—LOTS of them. (Cybersecurity loves them like toddlers love glitter.) But we'll also have stories, analogies, some light panic, and just enough sarcasm to keep your eyebrows raised while you learn to actually protect your digital kingdom.

You see, risk management in cybersecurity is like brushing your teeth. Everyone knows they should do it, some people fake it right before the check-up, and a few just ignore it until it hurts really, really bad. I'm here to help you become the person who flosses—digitally speaking, of course. Because ignoring cyber risks today is like living in Jurassic Park and pretending the fences will never go down.

Let's rewind a little.

When I started out in cybersecurity, I thought it was all about hacking tools and blinking terminals with green code. You know—The Matrix, hoodie-wearing geniuses, maybe a dark room with ominous techno music playing in the background. I was ready to dive into firewalls like Neo dodging bullets. But nope. What I walked into was risk assessments, compliance spreadsheets, endless emails about policies, and executive meetings where I had to explain to a C-level exec why "updating the router" doesn't just mean turning it off and back on again.

I learned the hard way that cybersecurity isn't just about stopping hackers—it's about managing uncertainty. It's about knowing where your systems are weakest, understanding which digital windows are open, and deciding whether to barricade them, board them up, or replace the entire building. It's about calculating what could go wrong, how bad it would be if it did, and how much duct tape we can afford to slap on it before the auditors scream.

This book is my attempt to take everything I've learned—through victories, mistakes, and the occasional existential breakdown—and turn it into something useful for you. Whether you're a newbie just trying to not break the network, a security lead juggling tools like flaming swords, or a CEO who Googled "cyber risk" and somehow landed here—there's something in this book for you.

We're going to walk through:

- How to identify threats, even the sneaky ones that don't wear hoodies.

- How to assess risks, without needing a PhD in paranoia.

- How to build mitigation strategies, so you're not playing whack-a-mole with malware.

- How to deal with third-party vendors, aka the people who leave the digital door open and let the raccoons in.

- How to respond when everything goes kaboom, and yes, sometimes it will.

And most importantly, how to make your organization cyber-resilient, which is just a fancy way of saying "tougher, smarter, and harder to break."

The chapters are designed so you can read them in order—or just skip to the part where your current problem lives. Need to convince your board you're not just the guy who says "no" to every cool new app? We've got a chapter for that. Need to know what to do when your backup gets encrypted and renamed "GiveMeBitcoin.zip"? Yup, covered.

Also, I promise to keep the tone light—because let's be honest, the world is already heavy enough. Cybersecurity should be serious, yes, but that doesn't mean it has to be soul-crushing. If I can make you laugh while you learn how to stop digital catastrophes, then my job here is done.

But I won't sugarcoat things either. The risks are real. The threats are evolving. And attackers? They don't take holidays. (I swear some of them work harder than I did during finals week.) Cyber risk management is not optional anymore. It's not something you tack onto your to-do list between buying coffee and updating the office printer driver. It's central. It's strategic. And yes—it can even be kind of fun, in a "solving-a-murder-mystery-while-defusing-a-bomb" sort of way.

So buckle up. This isn't a passive read. I'm going to make you think, maybe challenge some of your current approaches, and definitely make you rethink that one time you reused the same password for seven different accounts (you know who you are). I'll be your guide, your coach, your slightly snarky narrator, and occasionally your digital therapist.

Together, we're going to fortify, protect, and defend—your data, your organization, and hopefully your sanity. Because cyber risk management isn't just about technology—it's about people, choices, culture, and preparing for chaos with a cool head and a solid plan.

Welcome to the handbook.

Now let's get to work.

Chapter 1: Foundations of Cybersecurity Risk Management

You know that feeling when your email gets hacked, and suddenly your grandma is getting offers to invest in crypto from "you"? Yeah, that's the digital chaos we live in. Imagine running a business and that little email mishap turns into a multimillion-dollar data breach. Welcome to the wild world of cybersecurity risk—where everyone is a target, and clicking the wrong link is like stepping on a digital landmine. Let's rewind a bit, grab some virtual duct tape, and learn how this whole cyber risk thing came to be.

This chapter introduces the fundamental principles of cybersecurity risk management. It defines key terminology, traces the historical evolution of cyber threats, and explores why managing digital risk is not optional but essential. You'll get familiar with core frameworks like NIST, ISO 27005, and FAIR, and understand how these models provide the structure necessary for organizations to navigate the complex cybersecurity landscape.

1.1 Introduction to Cyber Risk

Alright, let's kick this off with a little honesty: when I first got into cyber security two decades ago, I thought it was all about firewalls, mysterious hackers in hoodies, and typing furiously while shouting "I'm in!" like in the movies. Spoiler alert: it's not like that. At all. Most of cyber security is far less glamorous and far more about managing risk—and a lot of coffee.

So buckle in, because understanding cyber risk is the bedrock of everything else in this handbook. You can't defend what you don't understand, and you definitely can't sleep at night if you don't know where the landmines are.

What Exactly is Cyber Risk?

Cyber risk is the possibility that a cyber threat will exploit a vulnerability and cause harm—financial loss, data theft, downtime, reputational damage, or even someone clicking a link they definitely shouldn't have. (Looking at you, Karen in Accounting.)

More formally, it's the intersection of:

- **Threats** (bad actors or events)
- **Vulnerabilities** (weak spots in systems/processes/people)
- **Assets** (things you care about protecting)

If those three things have a party together, you've got a cyber risk on your hands.

For example: if your company stores sensitive customer data (asset), but your employees use "password123" (vulnerability), and some cyber criminal is phishing around (threat), the risk is very real.

Cyber risk is not a "maybe someday" problem. It's an "every single day" reality. And it's getting weirder and wilder by the year.

Why Does Cyber Risk Matter?

Because modern life runs on tech. From banking to dating to ordering tacos —it's all digital. That means the attack surface (a fancy term for "stuff that can be hacked") keeps growing.

In the old days, your biggest worry was someone stealing a fax machine or glancing at confidential papers on your desk. Today? One click can give a stranger in another country full access to your business. One misconfigured cloud bucket can leak gigabytes of customer data. And ransomware? It's not just a buzzword—it's a billion-dollar criminal enterprise now.

Cyber risk management is no longer optional. It's a business imperative. Executives care. Regulators care. And trust me—your customers definitely care. No one wants their grandma's credit card leaked because someone forgot to patch a server.

Types of Cyber Risk (a.k.a. The Rogues Gallery)

Cyber risk isn't one-size-fits-all. Here are a few common flavors you'll run into:

- **Data Breach Risk** – When sensitive data gets exposed. This includes personal info (PII), health records, financial data, etc. Basically, the stuff you really don't want getting out.
- **Operational Risk** – When systems go down due to cyber incidents, like ransomware locking you out or a DDoS attack taking down your website. Oops.
- **Reputational Risk** – Trust takes years to build and seconds to destroy. Just ask any company that's had a high-profile hack.
- **Compliance Risk** – Ever heard of GDPR, HIPAA, or PCI-DSS? Yeah. Failing to protect data can lead to serious fines—and very grumpy legal departments.
- **Third-party Risk** – When your vendors or partners mess up and you pay the price. Because, of course, who doesn't love a cyber incident you didn't even cause?

It's like a box of chocolates —you never know what you're gonna get, but some of them might explode your infrastructure.

Common Threats That Lead to Cyber Risk

If cyber risk is the result, then threats are the cause. Here's what we're typically up against:

- **Phishing Attacks** – Emails pretending to be someone else, trying to get you to click, download, or share login details. Still ridiculously effective.
- **Malware** – Malicious software like ransomware, spyware, or keyloggers that sneak in and do bad things.
- **Insider Threats** – Employees or contractors (malicious or just careless) can pose huge risks.
- **Zero-day Exploits** – Attacks that use unknown software vulnerabilities before a patch exists.
- **Social Engineering** – When the "hack" isn't technical at all—it's psychological. Tricking people is still easier than breaking into a system.

Threat actors range from bored teenagers to state-sponsored cyber armies. That's not paranoia—it's reality.

How Do You Measure Cyber Risk?

This is where things get spicy because cyber risk isn't just about "Is there a risk?" It's about how much risk, and what can we do about it?

Most organizations use a risk equation like this:

Risk = Likelihood × Impact

- **Likelihood** – How likely is it that the threat will occur?

- **Impact** – What damage will it cause if it does?

For example, a DDoS attack might be likely but have low impact for some companies. But if you're a streaming platform and your service goes down for an hour? That's a six-figure disaster.

You'll also hear about qualitative vs quantitative risk assessments. In plain terms:

- **Qualitative** = Gut feeling + categories (high/medium/low)
- **Quantitative** = Numbers, dollars, charts

Both have their place. I'm personally a fan of putting dollar signs next to risks. Makes it easier to get management to actually listen.

Real Talk: You Can't Eliminate Risk

Here's the truth no one wants to put on a PowerPoint slide: you can't eliminate all cyber risk. It's impossible. The goal is to manage it.

We don't lock every door in a building with twelve deadbolts—we evaluate what's reasonable and adjust. Same goes for cyber security. It's about balancing cost, effort, and risk.

You mitigate some risks, accept others, transfer some via insurance, and try to stay sane in the process.

◈Risk Management Frameworks (Because Yes, There's a Process)

There are actual frameworks that help guide cyber risk decisions, such as:

- **NIST Risk Management Framework** (RMF)
- **ISO/IEC 27005**
- **FAIR** (Factor Analysis of Information Risk)

These aren't just alphabet soup—they help you think methodically about threats, vulnerabilities, and controls. Like IKEA instructions but for cyber defense. (Hopefully with fewer leftover screws.)

Final Thoughts: Risk is a Mindset

Understanding cyber risk isn't just for the CISO or the IT guy in the basement. Everyone—from interns to executives—has a role to play. Why? Because most breaches start with human error, not some elite hacker.

Think of cyber risk like driving a car. You wear a seatbelt, check your mirrors, lock the doors. Not because you're paranoid—but because you're being responsible.

Same thing here. Cyber risk management is just the adulting version of good digital hygiene.

And remember, just like pineapple on pizza —everyone has an opinion about what's risky. But at the end of the day, it's your job to assess it, own it, and manage it smartly.

1.2 Key Terminologies and Concepts

Before we get too deep into the cyber jungle, let's take a moment to learn the language of the land. Imagine trying to navigate Paris with zero French—"Bonjour, I'd like a cheeseburger, please?"—yeah, not fun. It's the same in cyber security. If you don't know the basic terms, you'll feel like you're drowning in a bowl of acronym alphabet soup.

But don't worry—I've got you. Here's your cheat sheet of key concepts and terms you'll hear all the time. And yes, some of them sound scarier than they are (others are way worse than they sound—yay).

Asset

Let's start easy: an asset is anything you care about protecting. Think data, hardware, software, intellectual property, customer trust, or even your CEO's secret cookie recipe

If losing it, breaking it, or exposing it would ruin your day (or year), it's an asset.

Vulnerability

A vulnerability is a weak spot in your system. Like leaving your front door open, or using "letmein123" as your admin password (yes, people still do this).

Vulnerabilities can be:

- **Technical** (e.g. unpatched software)
- **Human** (e.g. clicking phishing links)
- **Physical** (e.g. stolen laptops)

Patch them, fix them, train your people—just don't ignore them.

Threat

Now here's the drama: a threat is anything that could exploit a vulnerability and cause harm.

Threats include:

- Hackers
- Malware
- Natural disasters (yep, even a fire in the server room counts)
- Insider sabotage

Remember: threats are always out there. Some are just waiting for the right opportunity...like your outdated VPN server.

Threat Actor

These are the villains in our cyber story. They're the who behind the threats.

Types include:

- **Cybercriminals** – In it for the money
- **Hacktivists** – Political motives and edgy Twitter bios
- **Nation-State Actors** – Governments doing shady things
- **Script Kiddies** – Teenagers with free hacking tools and zero chill

No matter the flavor, they all spell trouble.

Attack Vector

This one sounds fancy, but it's just how the attack happens.

Common vectors:

- Phishing emails
- Malicious websites
- USB drives (still a thing!)
- Remote Desktop Protocol (RDP)

If it's a path from the bad guy to your stuff, it's an attack vector.

Control (a.k.a. Safeguard)

A control is anything you do to reduce risk.

Think of it like bug spray against mosquitoes. Controls include:

- Firewalls
- Strong passwords
- Security awareness training
- Antivirus software

Controls come in three delicious forms:

- **Preventive** – Keeps bad things from happening
- **Detective** – Tells you when bad things are happening
- **Corrective** – Helps you recover after something bad has happened

Use all three if you like sleeping at night.

Incident

An incident is what happens when a threat gets through your defenses. It could be:

- A ransomware attack that locks your files
- A data breach that exposes personal info
- A denial-of-service attack that crashes your website

When incidents happen, your job isn't to panic—it's to respond, recover, and learn.

And possibly cry a little. But just for a minute. Then back to work.

Risk

Ah yes, the star of the show! We covered this last chapter, but to recap:

- **Risk** = Likelihood × Impact

So, how likely is it that something bad will happen, and how bad would it be?

Risk is what connects threats, vulnerabilities, and assets together in one stressful equation.

Risk Assessment

This is the process of identifying and evaluating risks. Like a health check-up, but for your tech systems.

You'll ask:

- What are my assets?
- What could go wrong?
- How likely is it?
- How bad would it be?
- What am I doing about it?

Then document it. Rinse. Repeat. Preferably not on a sticky note.

Policy

Policies are your "rules of the road." They define how your organization should handle data, devices, access, and more.

For example:

- Acceptable Use Policy
- Password Policy

- Data Retention Policy

Boring? Maybe. But without them, it's the Wild West out here.

Response Plan

When the "oh no" moment hits, your incident response plan is what keeps you from flailing.

It should include:

- Who to call (not Ghostbusters)
- What steps to take
- How to contain and recover
- How to communicate

Having a plan > making it up as you go.

Security Awareness

Possibly your most underrated defense: people who know better.

Security awareness means your staff understand threats, know what to look out for, and don't click that sketchy "You've won a free iPhone" link.

Train your people like your business depends on it. Because it does.

A Quick Acronym Survival Kit

Let's decode some of the top offenders:

- **CIA Triad** – Confidentiality, Integrity, Availability
- **SOC** – Security Operations Center
- **SIEM** – Security Information and Event Management
- **IAM** – Identity and Access Management
- **MFA** – Multi-Factor Authentication
- **DLP** – Data Loss Prevention
- **APT** – Advanced Persistent Threat (a.k.a. the really scary kind of threat)

Learn these. Use them. Casually drop them in meetings to sound like a genius.

Final Thoughts: Speak Fluent Cyber

Understanding these terms isn't about sounding smart—it's about being effective. If you don't know the language, it's hard to fight the battles.

And let's be real: no one wants to be the person who nods along in a meeting while secretly Googling "what is a zero-day" under the table.

So now you've got the vocab, the vibe, and a little bit of sass to go with it. Onward to the next chapter—where we'll meet some of the bad guys up close. Don't worry, they're virtual. Probably.

1.3 Evolution of Cyber Threats

Ah, cyber threats—just like fashion trends and bad reality TV, they evolve... fast.

When I first dipped my toes into cyber security (cue nostalgic music), the threats were mostly virus-laden floppy disks and prank worms spreading through email. Fast-forward 20 years, and we're dealing with sophisticated ransomware gangs, AI-powered phishing, and hackers-for-hire operating like Fortune 500 companies. Yep, the bad guys grew up—and they got fancy.

So let's take a walk through time and see just how cyber threats have leveled up. It's like Pokémon evolution, but with more lawsuits and less Pikachu.

The Ancient Era (1970s–1980s): Curiosity Killed the Computer

Back in the digital stone age, threats were... kind of adorable. Hackers were mostly curious students, poking around networks because, well, they could. There wasn't much commercial internet, and most breaches were more about bragging rights than damage.

Key highlights:

- **Creeper Virus (1971):** Considered the first computer "virus." It didn't destroy anything—it just showed a message: "I'M THE CREEPER, CATCH ME IF YOU CAN!" Cute, right?
- **Elk Cloner (1982):** One of the first viruses in the wild, spreading via floppy disks. If you're too young to know what a floppy disk is, congrats—you're young.

These early threats were more like prank calls than actual crimes. But that innocence wouldn't last long...

The Growing Pains Era (1990s): Script Kiddies and Chaos

In the '90s, computers hit the mainstream and so did cyber threats. Suddenly, viruses weren't just jokes—they were destructive, fast-spreading, and annoying as hell.

Popular threats of the time:

- **Melissa (1999):** A virus that spread via Microsoft Word macros—because what's more dangerous than a document, right?
- **I LOVE YOU (2000):** A romantic-sounding email that wiped out files and spread itself to everyone in your address book. Talk about toxic relationships

This era gave birth to the infamous "script kiddies"—amateur hackers using downloadable tools without really understanding how they worked. Kind of like giving a toddler a chainsaw.

The Internet Boom Era (2000s): Malware Gets a Job

The 2000s were when cyber crime got... professional. No longer just for thrills, attackers were now after money, data, and power. Organized groups started to form, and attacks became more sophisticated.

Key trends:

- **Botnets:** Massive networks of infected devices, often used for spam or denial-of-service (DDoS) attacks. Zombie computers doing a hacker's bidding.

- **Spyware & Keyloggers:** Software that quietly logged every keystroke. "What could possibly go wrong?" –Everyone's password.

- **SQL Injection:** Attackers started targeting websites and databases to extract sensitive data. Because why go through the front door when you can exploit the backend?

And let's not forget the rise of phishing—a technique that tricked people into giving up passwords by pretending to be banks or Nigerian princes. (Still waiting on that inheritance, by the way.)

The Nation-State Era (2010s): Welcome to Cyber Cold War

Suddenly, cyber threats weren't just about criminals—they were about governments.

In this era, the gloves came off and state-sponsored cyber attacks became the new normal. Intelligence agencies were caught in digital turf wars, and companies found themselves caught in the crossfire.

Notable cases:

- **Stuxnet (2010):** A sophisticated worm allegedly created by the U.S. and Israel to sabotage Iran's nuclear program. It was the first known cyber weapon—and it changed the game.

- **Sony Hack (2014):** Allegedly orchestrated by North Korea, this attack exposed internal data, deleted systems, and even canceled a movie release.

- **Election Interference (2016):** We saw firsthand how cyber attacks could influence politics, spread misinformation, and erode public trust.

Cyber threats had officially entered the geopolitical stage. And with great power came great... terrifying consequences.

The Modern Era (2020s): Ransomware, AI, and Cyber-as-a-Service

Welcome to today. We live in an age where ransomware is a business model, hacking tools are sold on the dark web like Amazon deals, and artificial intelligence is both a tool and a threat.

Current trends:

- **Ransomware-as-a-Service (RaaS):** Yup, you can now subscribe to cybercrime platforms. Like Netflix, but with more extortion.

- **Double Extortion:** Attackers not only lock your files but threaten to leak them if you don't pay. A two-for-one special of panic!

- **Deepfake Phishing:** AI-generated voices and videos impersonate CEOs, tricking employees into wiring money or revealing credentials. "Yes, this is your boss. Totally legit. Now send that $50K."

- **Cloud & IoT Attacks:** As everything moves to the cloud and connects to the internet (hello, smart toasters), attackers follow. More devices = more risk.

And let's not forget the good ol' supply chain attacks—where threat actors compromise one vendor to reach dozens (or thousands) of victims. Think SolarWinds, MOVEit, and other headline-makers.

What's Next?

If I had a crystal ball, I'd probably be living on a beach somewhere instead of writing this chapter —but here's what we can expect:

- **More automation (on both sides)** – Attackers are getting faster, smarter, and lazier. They'll use AI to find vulnerabilities before you do.

- **Quantum computing threats** – Still early, but when quantum hits mainstream, it could break traditional encryption like a toothpick.

- **Cyber-physical attacks** – Think smart cars, hospitals, power grids. The real world and cyber world are merging. And when things go wrong, it's not just data at risk—it's lives.

Final Thoughts: From Script Kiddies to Cyber Cartels

We've gone from "look what I can do with a floppy disk" to ransomware gangs operating in broad daylight with PR reps. I'm not even joking—some of these groups run like startups. They've got help desks, branding, even affiliate programs.

But here's the thing: knowing how threats evolved helps us understand how to predict, prevent, and prepare for what's next.

Because while the tech changes, the core game stays the same: bad guys look for weaknesses. Good guys patch them. And in between, we drink a lot of coffee and try not to scream into the void.

1.4 Importance of Risk Management in Cybersecurity

Let me start with a bold (but true) statement:

Risk management is the unsung hero of cybersecurity.

It's not flashy. It doesn't involve cool gadgets, car chases, or yelling "I'm in!" while hacking a firewall like they do in movies. But without risk management, you're basically blindfolded, juggling chainsaws, on a tightrope, during a thunderstorm.

Okay, that might be dramatic—but you get the point.

Let's break down why risk management is so important, and why skipping it is like trying to assemble IKEA furniture without the instructions (and losing three screws in the carpet).

What Is Cyber Risk Management, Really?

In plain English: Risk management is the process of identifying, assessing, and responding to cyber risks before they ruin your day (or company).

Think of it like going to the doctor for a checkup—not because you're sick, but because you want to stay healthy. You're proactively looking for trouble spots, figuring out how bad they could get, and deciding what to do about them.

Cyber risk management does the same thing, but instead of cholesterol and blood pressure, you're watching for outdated systems, untrained staff, weak passwords, and that one guy in accounting who still thinks "123456" is acceptable.

Why It Actually Matters

Let's get real—security budgets aren't unlimited, and neither is time. You can't protect everything, everywhere, all the time. Risk management helps you:

- **Prioritize your resources**. Focus on the biggest, most likely threats.
- **Avoid surprises.** Know what's lurking in the shadows before it bites.
- **Improve decision-making.** You're making choices based on data, not vibes.
- **Stay compliant**. Regulations like GDPR, HIPAA, and others expect you to manage risks.
- **Build trust. Customers**, investors, and board members love a company that doesn't crumble under pressure.

It's not about creating a fortress. It's about knowing where the walls are thin—and reinforcing them before someone finds out the hard way.

Risk Management Is the Glue That Holds Everything Together

Here's a little secret from someone who's been in this field for two decades:

Most companies don't fall apart because of a single hack—they fall apart because they didn't know what to protect, or didn't take action when they did know.

Risk management is what ties your whole cybersecurity strategy together:

Function	How Risk Management Helps
Asset Management	Helps identify which systems/data matter most 🗂️📁
Access Control	Prioritizes who needs access to what 🔑
Incident Response	Prepares you for your most likely threats 🚨
Training & Awareness	Targets your biggest human risk factors 🧠

Without risk management, it's just a chaotic list of tools and policies with no strategy. Like a band with no drummer. Or a pizza with no cheese.(why would you even?)

The Money Talk: Cost of Ignoring Risk

Still not convinced? Okay, let's talk dollars.

Here's what ignoring cyber risk can cost you:

- **Data breaches:** $4.45 million average cost (according to IBM)
- **Ransomware payouts:** Hundreds of thousands—or millions—per incident
- **Downtime:** Thousands per minute for large companies
- **Regulatory fines:** GDPR alone can hit you with €20M fines
- **Reputation damage:** Priceless (in the worst way)

And don't forget the emotional cost of watching your boss stare at you like "How did this happen?" after the cyber hit.

Real-World Examples: When Risk Management Fails (Or Works!)

Failure: Equifax (2017)

One unpatched vulnerability. 147 million records exposed.

Why? Because nobody prioritized the patching process based on risk. A classic case of "we knew... but didn't act."

Success: Maersk (2017)

Hit hard by NotPetya malware. But thanks to solid planning and backups, they rebuilt their entire infrastructure within 10 days. That's what good risk management (and some IT heroics) can do.

It's Not a One-Time Thing

Here's the catch: risk management isn't a checklist you complete once and call it a day. It's a living process. The cyber threat landscape changes constantly—so should your risk strategy.

Remember:

- **New software?** New risks.
- **Company grows?** Risk grows.
- **Remote work?** Risks evolve.
- **AI tools?** You guessed it—new risks.

Cyber risk management is a dance. You're constantly adjusting your moves based on the rhythm of threats, tech, and business needs. Just don't forget to stretch.

Balance is Everything

Some folks think cyber security should be about locking everything down. No fun. No flexibility. Just all-out paranoia.

Others are like "Let's not worry about security until something breaks."

Risk management helps you find that sweet spot in the middle—secure enough to sleep at night, flexible enough to get work done.

Final Thoughts: Plan or Panic

Let me leave you with this little nugget of truth:

You can manage risk proactively... or reactively. One saves you money, the other saves you what's left of your job.

Risk management won't stop every breach, but it makes sure you're not caught off guard, unprepared, or pointing fingers in the middle of a crisis.

It's the grown-up part of cyber security. The strategic layer that separates the "we hope it never happens" from the "we're ready when it does."

So embrace it. Invest in it. And trust me—your future self (and your security team) will thank you.

1.5 Risk Management Frameworks Overview (NIST, ISO 27005, FAIR)

Let's be honest—risk management frameworks are kind of like gym memberships:

You know they're good for you, but actually using one takes motivation, a bit of pain, and possibly a spreadsheet or two.

But here's the deal: without a solid framework, your cyber risk program is like a GPS without a destination. You'll go somewhere, but probably not where you wanted.

So let me walk you through the three heavy-hitters in the cyber risk world—NIST, ISO 27005, and FAIR—in plain English, with just enough technical meat to impress your

CISO and keep your brain from melting.

1. NIST Risk Management Framework (RMF)

NIST is the U.S. government's go-to security playbook. It's the most structured of the bunch, which is both a blessing and a curse. If you like detailed checklists and federal-level security vibes, NIST is your BFF.

What It Is:

The NIST RMF (Risk Management Framework) guides organizations on how to categorize, select, implement, assess, authorize, and monitor information systems and their risks.

Sounds like a lot? Yeah, it kind of is. But it works.

The 7-Step RMF Process:

- **Prepare** – Set the stage (roles, responsibilities, risk tolerance)
- **Categorize** – What kind of data/system are we dealing with?
- **Select** – Choose the right security controls
- **Implement** – Put those controls into action
- **Assess** – Test them (don't just hope they work)
- **Authorize** – Management gives the thumbs-up
- **Monitor** – Rinse, repeat, improve

Who's It For?

- Government agencies
- Heavily regulated industries

- Security teams who love flowcharts

Real Talk:

NIST is like the IKEA of frameworks: very specific, with lots of steps, but if you follow the manual, you'll end up with a rock-solid risk strategy (and hopefully no leftover screws).

2. ISO/IEC 27005: Risk Management, International Style

ISO is basically the UN of cybersecurity frameworks. It's part of the larger ISO/IEC 27000 family, which includes everyone's favorite: ISO 27001 (for InfoSec management).

What It Is:

ISO/IEC 27005 provides a structured, yet flexible approach to information security risk management. It doesn't tell you what controls to implement—it tells you how to think about risk.

Think of it as your cybersecurity therapist.

The Core Steps:

1. **Context Establishment** – What does risk mean for you?
2. **Risk Identification** – What could go wrong?
3. **Risk Analysis** – How likely and how bad?
4. **Risk Evaluation** – What's worth acting on?
5. **Risk Treatment** – What will we do about it?
6. **Communication & Monitoring** – Keep everyone in the loop and eyes on the prize

Who's It For?

- Global organizations
- Companies aiming for ISO 27001 certification
- Teams wanting more flexibility

Real Talk:

ISO 27005 is like yoga: centered, holistic, adaptable. But if you're expecting a prescriptive to-do list... you might find yourself in child's pose wondering what to do next.

3. FAIR: Factor Analysis of Information Risk

Now for something completely different: FAIR is the only risk framework that puts a dollar sign on your risk. Yep—you can finally answer, "How much is this risk costing us?"

What It Is:

FAIR (Factor Analysis of Information Risk) is a quantitative risk analysis framework. It's focused on defining risk in terms of probability and financial impact, helping you make smart business decisions—not just tech ones.

Core Concepts:

- Risk = Frequency × Magnitude
- Uses terms like Loss Event Frequency, Threat Capability, Control Strength, and Loss Magnitude
- Built to support detailed risk modeling using real data, not just vibes

The Process (Simplified):

- **Define the scenario** – What's the risk event?
- **Evaluate probable frequency** – How often could this happen?
- **Estimate probable impact** – What would it cost us?
- **Analyze results** – Using simulation or math (yes, spreadsheets are involved)
- **Make decisions** – Invest where it matters

Who's It For?

- Risk analysts, CISOs, CFOs (who love numbers)
- Organizations tired of "high/medium/low" guessing games
- Decision-makers who want ROI clarity

Real Talk:

FAIR is the financial analyst of the bunch. It won't hold your hand through policy documents, but it will make you look really smart in front of your boss when you say, "This risk could cost us $2.4 million annually."

Quick Comparison Table

Feature	NIST RMF	ISO 27005	FAIR
Approach	Structured	Flexible	Quantitative
Origin	USA (Gov)	International	Private/Nonprofit
Focus	Controls & lifecycle	Risk process	Financial impact
Prescriptive?	Very	Somewhat	Not at all
Good For	Government, compliance	ISO 27001 users	Business decision-making
Easy to understand?	😬	😐	🤯

How to Choose the Right One?

Honestly? You don't have to pick just one.

These frameworks aren't mortal enemies—they can totally work together.

- Use NIST to build and monitor controls
- Use ISO 27005 to define your process
- Use FAIR to translate risk into $$$

Mix and match like cybersecurity tapas. Just don't try to implement all three at once with no plan—you'll overwhelm your team and burn out faster than a free VPN during a DDoS.

Final Thoughts: Frameworks Don't Fix Things—People Do

Here's the truth: A framework is only as good as the team using it. You can have the fanciest chart in the world, but if no one's actually applying it, it's just digital wallpaper.

Pick a framework (or combo) that fits your organization's size, maturity, and goals. Then actually use it—track risks, measure outcomes, improve constantly.

And most importantly... try not to fall asleep reading ISO documentation. Pro tip: espresso helps.

Chapter 2: Risk Identification and Threat Modeling

Imagine you're planning a heist movie, but instead of stealing diamonds, hackers are trying to steal your customer data. The first step in that movie? Scouting the target. That's risk identification! Whether it's the angry intern who still has VPN access or a rogue smart fridge sending spam, you've got to know what you're dealing with. Let's play detective—minus the trench coat and dramatic jazz soundtrack.

In this chapter, we delve into the process of identifying assets, evaluating potential threats, and modeling attack scenarios. You'll explore tools and techniques such as asset classification, vulnerability analysis, and structured threat modeling frameworks like STRIDE and DREAD. Understanding the nature of threats is essential for proactive cybersecurity risk mitigation.

2.1 Asset Identification and Classification

Alright, let's play a quick game:

Imagine you're the head of security at a museum.

Now answer this: Would you protect a clay coffee mug the same way you'd guard the

Mona Lisa?

Exactly. You'd slap lasers, guards, and 24/7 cameras on the priceless painting—and maybe just stick a "please don't touch" sign on the mug.

That's what asset identification and classification is all about:

Figuring out what you have, how important it is, and how much effort you should put into protecting it.

Simple in theory. In reality? A bit of a treasure hunt meets spreadsheet nightmare. But I'm here to help make it make sense.

What Is an "Asset" in Cybersecurity?

In cybersecurity terms, an asset is anything of value to your organization that could be affected by a cyber threat.

Think:

- **Hardware** – servers, laptops, IoT devices
- **Software** – applications, operating systems, licenses
- **Data** – customer records, financial data, trade secrets
- **People** – employees, contractors (yes, humans are assets—some more than others)
- **Networks** – internal infrastructure, cloud environments

If it's valuable, vulnerable, or vital to keeping the lights on—it's an asset.

Step 1: Asset Identification

Before you can protect something, you've got to know it exists. This is where most orgs already stumble.

Here's what makes this tricky:

- Assets are everywhere—cloud, on-prem, mobile, even smart fridges in break rooms (yes, it happens)
- Shadow IT is real—people spin up their own tools/services without telling IT (they just wanted to try that "free AI tool" real quick)

Remote work has scattered assets across home networks, coffee shops, and Airbnbs in Bali

Best Practices:

- **Asset inventory tools:** Use tools that automatically scan and list hardware/software
- **Collaboration with departments:** Talk to teams—don't rely on IT alone to "know everything"
- **Tag and track:** Assign IDs to assets. Treat them like Pokémon—you gotta catch 'em all

Step 2: Asset Classification

Okay, now that you've gathered your digital flock—it's time to sort the sheep from the gold-plated goats.

Asset classification means categorizing assets based on:

- Value to the organization
- Sensitivity of the information
- Impact if compromised

This helps you decide what gets the Fort Knox treatment... and what gets a polite pat on the head.

Typical Classifications:

High (Critical)

- **Think:** customer PII, payment info, source code
- **If lost or stolen** = disaster

Medium (Important)

- Think: internal reports, HR files, business emails
- Bad if compromised, but maybe not headline-worthy

Low (Non-sensitive)

- Think: marketing stock photos, cafeteria menu, Bob's meme folder
- You can sleep at night even if these go public

Bonus Tip: It's Not Forever

Assets change value over time! That startup idea on a napkin? If it becomes your next product... that napkin just became high-value IP.

Why This Matters: Security Ain't Free

Cybersecurity isn't one-size-fits-all. If you try to protect everything like it's nuclear launch codes, two things will happen:

1. You'll go broke.
2. Your users will revolt over constant MFA and network scans

Classification lets you focus protection where it counts.

- **High-value assets?** → Encrypt, monitor, limit access, and back them up daily.
- **Low-value assets?** → Maybe just basic antivirus and logging.

Smart security is strategic, not paranoid.

Real-World Oops Moments

Let's take a walk down memory lane, shall we?

The Unlabeled Database

An e-commerce company left a cloud-hosted customer database unencrypted and exposed. Why?

Nobody knew it existed. It wasn't even listed in their inventory. Boom—5 million customer records gone. Ouch.

Classify Like a Boss

A healthcare org implemented strict classification for patient records, R&D files, and vendor contracts.

When ransomware hit? Their most critical data was safely backed up and encrypted. Business disruption = minimal.

Tools to Help You Not Go Crazy

You're probably thinking, "How am I supposed to find and classify everything?"

Good news—you're not alone. There are tools for this.

- **CMDBs** (Configuration Management Databases) – For centralized asset records
- **Asset Discovery Tools** – Like Qualys, Tenable, or Rapid7
- **Cloud Inventory Managers** – AWS Config, Azure Resource Graph, etc.
- **Data Discovery Tools** – Helps locate and classify sensitive files

And remember: Automation is your friend. Because doing this all in spreadsheets? That way lies madness.

Wrap-Up: Know Thy Stuff

At the end of the day, cybersecurity without asset identification is like putting a security system in a house... but forgetting where the doors and windows are.

You have to know:

- What you own
- Where it lives
- Why it matters
- What could go wrong if it's compromised

Start there, and suddenly the rest of your security strategy starts making sense. It's not just throwing firewalls around at random—it's intentional protection based on value.

Final Thoughts: Don't Be the "Oops, I Forgot We Owned That" Company

If you walk away with one thing, let it be this:

You can't protect what you don't know exists.

And believe me, nothing makes a security team sweat faster than finding out their "totally secure" system has been missing a major asset the whole time.

So go forth, audit your assets, tag your tech, and maybe finally get Bob to delete his 2012 meme archive. For security, of course.

2.2 Threat Intelligence Sources and Tools

If I had a dollar for every time someone said, "We had no idea that was coming," after a cyberattack... well, I'd be typing this from a beach in the Maldives.

But seriously—threat intelligence is your early warning system in the cyber world. It's like knowing which streets to avoid because a gang of ransomware bandits is hanging out with DDoS hooligans around the corner.

So, buckle up. In this chapter, we're diving into where to find cyber threat info, how to use it, and what tools can help—without turning you into a full-time threat analyst (unless that's your thing, in which case, respect).

What is Threat Intelligence, Really?

At its core, threat intelligence is information that helps you understand:

- Who might attack you
- Why they might do it
- How they'd do it
- What you can do about it

It's like cybersecurity with insider gossip. But instead of office drama, it's about malware strains, attack vectors, and shady forums on the dark web.

Types of Threat Intelligence

Threat intel isn't one-size-fits-all. It comes in different flavors based on how it's used and how detailed it is.

1. Strategic Threat Intelligence

High-level stuff for the execs—what nation-states or big threat groups are up to.

- *"APT29 is targeting healthcare again."*
- *"Ransomware attacks in finance are up 35%."*

Good for: C-suite, board members, long-term planning

Not so good for: Telling you what file to block right now

2. Tactical Threat Intelligence

Details on the TTPs (Tactics, Techniques, and Procedures) used by attackers.

- How phishing emails are bypassing spam filters
- Malware obfuscation methods

Good for: SOC teams, red/blue teams

Not for: High-level business strategy

3. Operational Threat Intelligence

Real-time info about specific incoming attacks.

- "IP 45.129.201.99 is scanning your firewall RIGHT NOW."
- "This zero-day is being exploited in the wild."

Good for: Immediate incident response

Not for: Trend reports or long-term risk analysis

4. Technical Threat Intelligence

- Nitty-gritty stuff like IOCs (Indicators of Compromise)—IP addresses, hashes, URLs.
- MD5 hash of known malware
- Suspicious domain names

Good for: SIEMs, firewalls, endpoint protection

Not for: Humans without coffee

Threat Intelligence Sources: Where the Good Stuff Lives

Now that we know what threat intel is, let's talk about where to get it. You've got a buffet of sources—free, paid, internal, and external.

Free/Open-Source Threat Intel (OSINT)

AlienVault OTX (Open Threat Exchange)

Community-driven threat intel sharing. Think Reddit meets threat feeds.

https://otx.alienvault.com/

AbuseIPDB

A crowd-sourced database of bad IPs. Helps you spot known troublemakers.

https://www.abuseipdb.com/

VirusTotal

Upload a file, URL, or hash and see what 70+ AV engines think.

https://www.virustotal.com/

MITRE ATT&CK Framework

A treasure map of attacker techniques and tools. Essential reading.

https://attack.mitre.org/

Have I Been Pwned?

Great for checking if your email (or your boss's) was part of a breach.

https://haveibeenpwned.com/

Commercial Threat Intel Platforms

If you've got budget, these platforms serve up curated, real-time intel that can integrate with your tech stack:

- **Recorded Future** – AI-powered intel across all levels
- **ThreatConnect** – Threat intel + risk management
- **Anomali** – Great for aggregating multiple feeds
- **CrowdStrike Falcon X** – If you're already using CrowdStrike EDR, this one's a gem
- **Mandiant Threat Intelligence** – Top-tier threat actor profiles and insights

Pro tip: Don't buy intel just to "check a box." Make sure it integrates with your tools and aligns with your threat model.

Threat Intelligence Tools: From Manual to Magic

You don't have to process all this intel manually (unless you enjoy pain). These tools can automate, organize, and act on threat info.

TIPs (Threat Intelligence Platforms)

- Organize, enrich, and share intel internally
- Examples: MISP (open-source), ThreatConnect, Anomali

SIEMs (Security Information and Event Management)

- Use threat intel to detect and respond to incidents
- Examples: Splunk, LogRhythm, Microsoft Sentinel

SOAR (Security Orchestration, Automation, and Response)

- Automatically block threats or isolate assets based on intel
- Examples: Palo Alto Cortex XSOAR, IBM Resilient

Firewalls & EDRs

- Many next-gen solutions ingest threat feeds to dynamically block IOCs
- Examples: Fortinet, CrowdStrike, SentinelOne

Use Case: From Threat Intel to Action

Let's say your threat feed flags a suspicious domain tied to phishing attacks.

Here's how good threat intel turns into real protection:

1. Your TIP ingests the IOC (domain).
2. SIEM correlates it with recent DNS logs.
3. SOAR triggers an alert + blocks the domain via firewall.
4. EDR isolates any endpoint that tried to visit it.
5. You look like a cybersecurity rockstar.

The Big Mistake: Drowning in Data

Here's a harsh truth: More threat intel doesn't always mean better security.

If you're collecting 3,000 IOCs per day and acting on none of them... that's not threat intelligence. That's just digital hoarding.

The key? Prioritize and contextualize.

Focus on what's relevant to your industry, your assets, and your environment.

Because while it's cool to know North Korean hackers are targeting aerospace firms... that won't help you much if you're running an e-commerce site in Texas.

Final Thoughts: Intelligence is Power (Only If You Use It)

Threat intelligence is your early warning system, your radar, your cyber crystal ball —but only if you actually use it.

- Set up your sources
- Integrate your tools
- Act on what matters

Otherwise, you're just collecting spooky trivia—and while that's fun, it won't keep your servers safe at 3 a.m.

And hey, if nothing else, knowing the hash of the latest malware strain makes for killer small talk at nerdy dinner parties.

2.3 Vulnerability Scanning and Analysis

Let's kick this off with a hard truth:

"You're never fully patched. You're just between vulnerabilities."

Yup. The second you update one thing, something else screams for attention. It's like playing cyber whack-a-mole, but the moles are critical security flaws and you're holding a foam hammer.

That's why vulnerability scanning and analysis is such a crucial part of your security routine. It's not glamorous. It doesn't get movie cameos. But it's the difference between "we found it first" and "we're in the headlines for all the wrong reasons."

Let's dive in.

What is a Vulnerability?

A vulnerability is a weakness in your system that could be exploited by an attacker.

Think of it like:

- An unlocked window on the 1st floor
- A door with a broken deadbolt
- That intern who insists on using "Password123" everywhere

Vulnerabilities can exist in:

- Operating systems (Windows, Linux)
- Applications (web servers, CMS platforms)
- Network devices (routers, firewalls)
- Even misconfigurations or weak policies

If it can be exploited—intentionally or accidentally—it's a vulnerability.

What is Vulnerability Scanning?

Vulnerability scanning is the process of automatically probing your systems to identify known security weaknesses.

Imagine hiring a robot to walk around your digital building, jiggling every doorknob, peeking into vents, and testing windows—then giving you a report of what it found.

It's not exploitation. That's pen testing. This is just scanning—like a check-up at the doctor's office. No scalpels, just a thermometer and some awkward questions.

Types of Vulnerability Scans

Depending on your needs and paranoia level, you've got a few flavors of scans to choose from:

Network Scans

- Target: IP ranges, routers, servers
- Goal: Find open ports, outdated firmware, weak services
- Used in both internal and external scans

Host-Based Scans

- Target: Individual devices (laptops, servers)
- Checks patch levels, configurations, and file systems

Application Scans

- Target: Web apps, APIs
- Finds SQL injection, XSS, and other OWASP Top 10 flaws

Wireless Scans

- Target: Wi-Fi networks and access points
- Looks for rogue devices or weak encryption

Cloud Scans

- Target: AWS, Azure, GCP environments
- Checks for misconfigurations (like wide-open S3 buckets)

Authenticated vs. Unauthenticated Scans

Quick distinction:

- **Unauthenticated Scan:** Outsider perspective. Like checking your house by peeking through the windows.
- **Authenticated Scan:** Insider view. Like being let in with a key to check under the couch cushions.

Authenticated scans give way more accurate results—but also require more setup. It's worth the effort though, unless you enjoy false positives and incomplete reports.

Top Vulnerability Scanning Tools

Here's your toolbox. Pick wisely.

Open Source / Freemium:

- **OpenVAS (Greenbone)** – Great free scanner for networks and systems.
- **Nmap + NSE Scripts** – Not technically a vulnerability scanner, but with the right scripts? Super handy.
- **Nikto** – Web server scanner. Old-school but reliable.

Commercial Tools:

- **Nessus** – Popular, powerful, user-friendly. A classic.
- **Qualys** – Cloud-based scanning with strong compliance features.
- **Rapid7 InsightVM (formerly Nexpose)** – Good visual reporting and integrations.
- **Tenable.io** – The SaaS version of Nessus with more bells and whistles.
- **Burp Suite (Pro)** – Web application scanning powerhouse.

Each has strengths and quirks—test a few if you can. Your environment and budget will help decide the best fit.

Understanding the Output: Reading a Scan Report Without Crying

Scan done? Great. Now prepare for a wall of alerts.

Most reports will give you:

- **CVE ID** – The official name of the vulnerability (e.g., CVE-2023-12345)
- **Severity** – Usually scored using CVSS (Common Vulnerability Scoring System)
- **0–3.9:** Low
- **4–6.9:** Medium
- **7–8.9:** High
- **9–10:** Critical
- **Description** – What the vulnerability is and why it's bad
- **Fix Recommendations** – Patch info, config changes, etc.

Pro Tip: Don't panic if your scan shows hundreds of vulnerabilities. Prioritize:

1. Critical + exploited in the wild
2. High-risk + internet-facing
3. Chained vulnerabilities (low ones that can be combined to create big problems)

How Often Should You Scan?

Ideal world? Continuous scanning.

Real world? Try:

- Monthly for internal systems
- Weekly or daily for external-facing apps
- After any major change (e.g., new deployment, patch rollout)
- Before audits—trust me on this one

Automated scans + regular schedules = one less thing to lose sleep over.

Vulnerability Analysis: Don't Just Find It, Understand It

Scanning alone doesn't equal security. The analysis part is what separates a checkbox exercise from actual risk reduction.

Ask yourself:

- Is this vulnerability reachable by an attacker?
- Can it be chained with another to escalate privileges?
- Is there a known exploit available?
- Does this system store sensitive data?

This context turns a boring list of CVEs into a prioritized roadmap for your security team.

Also: Check if your scanner cries wolf. Some tools overreport—don't waste time chasing ghosts.

Real-World Example: The Lazy Patch

A company discovered a critical remote code execution vulnerability on a public web server (via Nessus). They marked it "low priority" because "nobody uses that system anymore."

A few weeks later? That same system got popped, the attacker pivoted inside the network, and ransomware took out production. Cost: $2.7 million.

Moral of the story: if it's critical, patch it—even if you think it's "not important."

Vulnerability Management ≠ Patch Everything

Spoiler alert: You don't need to fix every single vulnerability right away. You just need to fix:

- The ones that actually matter
- The ones that expose your crown jewels
- The ones that could be automated or easily exploited

Combine scanning with asset classification, threat intel, and risk assessment, and suddenly your patching priorities become much clearer.

Final Thoughts: Scan Like Nobody's Watching, Patch Like Everyone Is

Vulnerability scanning isn't sexy, but it's essential.

It's like flossing for your network—if you don't do it, eventually things rot and fall out.

So schedule your scans, tune your tools, and make friends with your patching team (bribe them with snacks if needed).

And remember: no scanner is perfect. But having one is a heck of a lot better than finding out about your vulnerabilities from a ransom note.

2.4 Threat Modeling Techniques (STRIDE, DREAD, PASTA)

Ever tried to fix something before it breaks? Welcome to the beautiful world of threat modeling—aka thinking like a hacker before they do.

It's kind of like planning for a zombie apocalypse: you don't want it to happen, but if it does, you'd rather not be the guy Googling "how to barricade a door" mid-bite.

In this chapter, we're diving into the three most common and battle-tested threat modeling approaches: STRIDE, DREAD, and PASTA. No, these aren't hacker aliases (though I'd totally join a hacker group named "PASTA").

Let's get threat-intelligent, shall we?

First, What the Heck is Threat Modeling?

At its core, threat modeling is:

A structured process to identify, evaluate, and prioritize potential threats to your system.

You basically ask:

- What are we building?
- What could go wrong?
- What are we doing about it?
- Did we do a good job?

Think of it like a brainstorming session with anxiety issues. But productive.

STRIDE: Microsoft's Oldie but Goodie

STRIDE was cooked up by Microsoft in the 1990s. And despite its age, it's still relevant—like the "Don't Talk to Strangers" of threat modeling.

Each letter represents a type of threat:

Letter	Threat Type	What It Means
S	Spoofing	Pretending to be someone else
T	Tampering	Messing with data or code
R	Repudiation	Denying actions (e.g., "I didn't do that!")
I	Information Disclosure	Leaking sensitive info
D	Denial of Service	Making something unavailable (DoS/DDoS)
E	Elevation of Privilege	Gaining unauthorized access

How to Use STRIDE:

1. Diagram your system (data flows, users, trust boundaries)
2. Walk through each element and ask: "Could someone spoof here? Tamper? Leak data?"
3. Document the threats, plan mitigations.

Pro Tip: STRIDE works great during design phases. Pair it with tools like Microsoft's Threat Modeling Tool to automate the fun.

Example:

In an online banking app:

- **Spoofing:** Hacker pretends to be a legit user.
- **Tampering:** Alters transaction data in transit.
- **Information Disclosure:** Sensitive account info leaks via logs.

STRIDE may be old, but like a grandpa with a shotgun—it still gets the job done.

DREAD: Rating the "Oh Crap" Factor

DREAD is all about prioritization. It lets you assign scores to threats so you can sort the "fix it now!" from the "meh, someday maybe."

Letter	What It Measures
D	Damage Potential
R	Reproducibility
E	Exploitability
A	Affected Users
D	Discoverability

Each gets a score from 1–10. Add 'em up, divide by 5, and boom: you've got a threat severity rating.

Example: SQL Injection on Login Page

Metric	Score (1–10)
Damage	9
Reproducibility	10
Exploitability	8
Affected Users	9
Discoverability	7

Average Score: 8.6

That's a red alert, my friend.

When to Use DREAD:

- Post-STRIDE, when you've identified threats and now want to prioritize
- During risk analysis and sprint planning

Warning: Some orgs shy away from DREAD because scoring can get subjective. One person's "minor inconvenience" is another's "career-ending breach."

PASTA: The Deliciously Serious Framework

PASTA stands for:

- Process for Attack Simulation and Threat Analysis
- And no, unfortunately, it doesn't involve spaghetti.

PASTA is a full-blown, 7-stage threat modeling framework that's all about aligning security with business impact.

The 7 Stages of PASTA:

Define the Business Objectives

What are we protecting and why?

Define the Technical Scope

Map out the tech stack, architecture, boundaries.

Decompose the Application

Dig deep into components, data flows, roles.

Analyze Threats

Use STRIDE, MITRE ATT&CK, etc.

Analyze Vulnerabilities

Add results from vuln scanning, pen tests.

Analyze Attacks

Simulate attack paths, identify choke points.

Risk & Impact Analysis

Tie threats to business impact and prioritize.

PASTA = STRIDE + DREAD + Business Brain

Use this if you:

- Need a risk-driven model (think: financial services, healthcare)
- Want to simulate attack paths and assess real-world business impact
- Love charts, workflows, and frameworks (you spreadsheet freak, you)

STRIDE vs. DREAD vs. PASTA: Fight Night

Feature	STRIDE	DREAD	PASTA
Focus	Threat types	Threat severity	Full attack simulation
When to Use	Design phase	Prioritization	Risk-heavy industries
Complexity	Low–Medium	Medium	High
Business Impact?	Not directly	Somewhat	Strongly aligned
Works with Others?	DREAD, PASTA	STRIDE, PASTA	Integrates both

Real-Life Example: Why Threat Modeling Saves Bacon

Company launches new mobile app. No threat modeling. No STRIDE, no PASTA, not even a whiff of DREAD.

Three weeks in, attackers spoof a user session, tamper with backend requests, and pull personal data from 10,000 users.

Post-breach audit reveals:

- No input validation (oops)
- No logging or non-repudiation (uh-oh)
- No threat modeling (facepalm)

Cost: Legal fees, compliance fines, user trust, and someone's job.

◈ Final Thoughts: Model Before You Build (or Regret)

Threat modeling is like flossing for developers and security teams:

- It's annoying at first.
- It's easy to skip.
- But skip it enough... and everything falls apart.

So whether you go for STRIDE's checklist, DREAD's scoring system, or PASTA's full-course experience, just start modeling.

Because the only thing worse than getting hacked... is realizing you could've predicted it with 30 minutes and a whiteboard.

2.5 Case Studies in Threat Identification

"Learn from the mistakes of others. You won't live long enough to make them all yourself." – Someone wise and probably breached

Welcome to the chapter where we look at how threat identification works in real life — beyond the whiteboards and buzzwords.

Because let's be honest: nothing drives a security point home like a real-world "oops."

Whether it's a massive data leak or a clever exploit no one saw coming, there's always something valuable to learn.

So buckle up — we're diving into some case studies that will make you smarter... and maybe just a little paranoid.

Case Study 1: Capital One & The Leaky AWS Bucket

- **Year:** 2019
- **Industry:** Finance
- **Threat Type**: Misconfiguration, Insider Threat

What Happened?

A former AWS employee exploited a misconfigured web application firewall (WAF) to access sensitive Capital One data stored in AWS S3 buckets.

The attacker used a server-side request forgery (SSRF) to obtain credentials from the metadata service, pivot into the environment, and download personal data of over 100 million users.

Threats Missed:

- SSRF vulnerability not modeled or mitigated
- Overly broad permissions in IAM roles
- Misconfigured S3 buckets (those buckets just love spilling secrets)

Lessons Learned:

- Include cloud-specific threats in your modeling (hello STRIDE and PASTA)
- Don't sleep on insider knowledge as a threat
- Regularly audit IAM roles and access permissions

Bonus:

The attacker bragged about the breach on GitHub. That's right — GitHub. Talk about leaving receipts.

Case Study 2: Equifax – The One That Haunts Us All

- **Year:** 2017
- **Industry:** Credit Reporting
- **Threat Type:** Known Vulnerability Exploited

What Happened?

Attackers exploited a known vulnerability in Apache Struts (CVE-2017-5638) to gain access to Equifax's systems and steal data from 147 million Americans.

They had months to patch it... but didn't.

Threats Missed:

- Failure to identify a public, critical vulnerability
- No automated threat intel feeds for patch alerts
- No real-time vulnerability prioritization

Lessons Learned:

- Threat identification isn't just about new attacks — old flaws matter too
- Integrate threat intelligence sources with vulnerability scanning
- If a vulnerability has a CVE and a working exploit, patch it like your job depends on it (because it probably does)

Case Study 3: SolarWinds – The Update That Betrayed

- **Year:** 2020
- **Industry:** IT / National Security
- **Threat Type:** Advanced Persistent Threat (APT), Supply Chain Attack

What Happened?

State-sponsored attackers inserted malware ("SUNBURST") into a routine software update for SolarWinds' Orion platform. The poisoned update was then distributed to 18,000+ customers, including U.S. government agencies.

That's like a Trojan Horse in the shape of a software patch.

Threats Missed:

- No modeling for supply chain threats

- No code integrity checks on updates
- Lack of anomaly detection on outbound traffic from trusted tools

Lessons Learned:

- Threat identification must now include 3rd-party code and vendors
- Build a zero trust architecture — don't assume internal = safe
- Monitor even "trusted" systems for suspicious activity

Bonus Insight:

The attackers were in the systems for months before being discovered. That's a very slow-moving nightmare.

Case Study 4: Uber – The Gift That Kept Giving

- **Year:** 2022
- **Industry:** Ride Sharing
- **Threat Type:** Social Engineering + MFA Fatigue

What Happened?

A teen(!) used social engineering to compromise an Uber contractor's credentials. Then they spammed MFA requests until the contractor finally hit "approve" out of sheer annoyance.

Yes. The attack was basically:

"Let's bug them into submission."

Once in, they accessed internal tools, code, and more — then bragged about it on Uber's Slack.

Threats Missed:

- No defense against MFA fatigue
- Poor internal segmentation (lateral movement was too easy)
- No modeling for non-technical, social attack vectors

Lessons Learned:

- **MFA is awesome** — until attackers weaponize it
- **Use smarter auth:** FIDO2, push MFA with geofencing, or MFA context-aware rules
- **Include human-centric threats in your modeling** — because users be users

Case Study 5: Target – A Chilly Entry Point

- **Year:** 2013
- **Industry:** Retail
- **Threat Type:** Third-Party Compromise

What Happened?

Attackers stole credentials from an HVAC contractor (yes, air conditioning), which they used to access Target's network. From there, they installed malware on point-of-sale (POS) systems and harvested 40 million credit card numbers.

Threats Missed:

- No third-party access control modeling
- Weak network segmentation
- No monitoring for weird internal traffic from HVAC vendor to POS systems

Lessons Learned:

- Threat models should include every vendor and contractor
- Least privilege access isn't a suggestion — it's a survival tactic
- Network segmentation saves lives. And credit card numbers.

Threat Identification Takeaways

Across all these case studies, some themes emerge louder than a breached alert siren:

- **Threats come from everywhere** – external, internal, third-party, even your HVAC guy.
- **Threat modeling isn't just a paper exercise** – it's a survival strategy.
- **Automation helps** – but humans still need to think critically about how systems can be abused.
- **Old flaws still kill** – don't ignore something just because it's not shiny and new.
- **Paranoia pays off** – model more threats than you think you need to. Odds are, one of them will happen.

Final Thoughts: Don't Be the Next Case Study

These case studies aren't here to scare you (okay, maybe a little). They're here to remind you that threat identification is real, messy, and ongoing.

Your systems aren't safe because you ran a scanner once or checked a box on a compliance form. They're safe when you constantly ask:

"What could go wrong?" ...and then build to stop it.

And hey — if you ever feel like you're being overly cautious, just remember:

At least you're not the guy who got hacked through the air conditioner.

Chapter 3: Risk Assessment and Prioritization

Okay, you've found the skeletons in your digital closet—now what? You don't panic, you rank! Like deciding whether to rescue your phone from a puddle or stop your cat from chewing a power cable, not all risks are created equal. Let's roll up our sleeves and figure out which fires to put out first (and which ones we can just fan a little).

This chapter covers the principles of assessing cyber risks in a structured manner. You'll learn how to analyze both the likelihood and impact of identified threats, apply quantitative and qualitative methodologies, and prioritize them effectively using risk matrices, the CVSS scoring system, and the FAIR model. The goal is to focus limited resources on the most pressing vulnerabilities.

3.1 Quantitative vs Qualitative Risk Assessments

Let's start with a universal truth:

Risk is everywhere, and somehow, we're supposed to measure it.

But how do you measure something like the risk of your CFO clicking a malicious link because it looked like an urgent pizza order?

Welcome to the world of risk assessment, where you can either:

- **Assign risks hard numbers** (quantitative), or
- **Use categories and judgment** (qualitative)

Spoiler: Both have pros, cons, and a healthy dose of "it depends."

Quantitative Risk Assessment: Crunching the Cold, Hard Numbers

Quantitative assessments aim to answer the question:

"How much will it cost us if this threat happens?"

We use data, probabilities, and math. Yep — the kind with formulas. If you're the type who actually uses Excel's =VLOOKUP, this one's for you.

Key Metrics:

SLE (Single Loss Expectancy)

= Asset Value × Exposure Factor

→ *"How much do we lose each time this threat hits?"*

ARO (Annualized Rate of Occurrence)

→ *"How often does this happen per year?"*

ALE (Annualized Loss Expectancy)

= SLE × ARO

→ *"How much are we expected to lose yearly?"*

Example:

Let's say:

- **Asset:** Customer DB worth $1,000,000

- **Exposure Factor:** 0.4 (we'd lose 40% of its value if breached)
- **ARO:** 0.5 (happens every 2 years)

Then:

- **SLE** = $1,000,000 × 0.4 = $400,000
- **ALE** = $400,000 × 0.5 = $200,000/year

Boom! Now you can walk into a boardroom and say,

"This risk is costing us $200K a year — let's do something about it."

Pros:

- Data-driven decisions
- Easy to compare ROI on security controls
- Useful for budget justification (CFOs love it)

Cons:

- Requires accurate data (which is often rare)
- Risk is not always measurable (like reputational damage)
- Math doesn't work well with unicorn threats

Qualitative Risk Assessment: Art Meets Cybersecurity

This method is like judging a risk by its vibe — but with a little structure.

Instead of numbers, risks are rated based on:

- Likelihood (Low / Medium / High)
- Impact (Low / Medium / High)
- Combined into a handy matrix

Risk Matrix:

	Low Impact	Medium Impact	High Impact
Low Likelihood	Low	Low	Medium
Medium Likelihood	Low	Medium	High
High Likelihood	Medium	High	Critical

Example:

A phishing attack targeting marketing staff:

- **Likelihood:** High (they get a lot of email)
- **Impact:** Medium (not customer-facing)

→ **Risk Rating: High**

No math. No spreadsheets. Just color-coded danger zones.

Pros:

- Easy to use and explain to non-tech folks
- Great for brainstorming and workshops
- Doesn't require precise data

Cons:

- Subjective (Bob says "high"; Alice says "meh")
- Hard to track over time
- Less helpful for financial planning or insurance

Quantitative vs Qualitative: The Cyber Smackdown

Feature	Quantitative 📊	Qualitative 🧠
Based on	Numbers, math	Experience, judgment
Outputs	Dollar values, ALE	Risk categories
Good for	ROI, budgeting	Quick assessments
Data requirement	High	Low
Flexibility	Low	High
Boardroom appeal	Very High	Medium-ish
Analyst burnout potential	Also very high 😫	Mild 😌

TL;DR:

- If you have reliable data → go quantitative
- If you're just starting, or need a broad overview → go qualitative
- If you want the best of both worlds? Use hybrid

The Hybrid Approach (aka, the Reasonable Adult Option)

Most mature organizations don't choose just one. Instead, they:

- Start qualitative to identify top risks
- Go quantitative for the highest priorities

That way, you don't waste time doing ALE math on "website font mismatch" risk, but you do quantify what a ransomware incident could cost you.

The hybrid method lets you scale your efforts as the business matures. It's the cybersecurity version of going from training wheels to a full-blown Ducati.

When to Use What?

Situation	Best Approach
Small business, no data?	Qualitative
Justify budget to executives?	Quantitative
Large enterprise, tons of data?	Quantitative + Hybrid
Fast risk snapshot?	Qualitative
Long-term security planning?	Quantitative / Hybrid

Final Thoughts: Risk Is Like Salsa

Some people want it mild (just enough info to decide),

Some want it burn-your-soul-off spicy (detailed models, full quant),

But either way — you better have some on the table.

Whether you're using numbers or gut feelings, the goal is the same:

→ Know what can go wrong

→ Know how bad it could be

→ Know what you're gonna do about it

And remember:

Guessing is not a strategy. But informed guessing? Now we're getting somewhere.

3.2 Impact and Likelihood Analysis

"What's the worst that could happen?"

— Every cybersecurity person, 15 seconds before the SIEM explodes

Welcome to the meat and potatoes of risk assessment: figuring out not just what could go wrong, but how likely it is and how bad it would be if it did. It's basically the "choose your own disaster" section of the book.

At the heart of every cyber risk decision lies two magic ingredients:

- Impact (How bad is it?)
- Likelihood (How often will it happen?)

Mix those two, and voilà — you've got yourself a risk rating. Let's dig in.

Likelihood: Will It Happen or Nah?

Likelihood is the probability that a specific threat will successfully exploit a vulnerability within a given timeframe. In less nerdy terms:

"How likely is this digital dumpster fire?"

Factors that affect likelihood:

- **Threat actor capability** (Script kiddie vs nation-state)
- **Exposure level** (Is it internet-facing?)
- **Vulnerability presence** (Is there a juicy bug to exploit?)
- **Control strength** (Are your defenses up to snuff?)

Likelihood Scales:

- **Quantitative:** Probability values like 0.1 (10%) or 0.75 (75%)
- **Qualitative:** Labels like "Low," "Medium," "High," or "Almost certain"

Real-World Example:

- **A phishing email to your entire company?** High likelihood.
- **An APT using a zero-day on your fax machine?** Unlikely (unless you're a secret agent from 1995).

Impact: If It Hits, How Hard?

Impact is what happens when things go sideways. It's the consequence of a successful attack. The bigger the blast radius, the higher the impact.

Types of Impact:

- **Financial** – Cost of downtime, recovery, fines
- **Operational** – Disruption to services or production
- **Reputational** – Media backlash, customer trust loss
- **Legal/Compliance** – Regulatory penalties
- **Safety** – Physical harm (especially in OT environments)

Impact Scales:

- **Quantitative:** Dollar values ("This breach could cost $3M")
- **Qualitative:** Labels ("Minor," "Moderate," "Severe," "Catastrophic")

Real-World Example:

- A ransomware attack shutting down a hospital? Catastrophic impact.
- A defaced marketing blog post? Eh... low impact (unless your blog was how you sold life-saving medicine).

Combining Impact + Likelihood = Risk Rating

Now here's where the magic happens. By mapping impact and likelihood together, you get a risk level.

Most orgs use a risk matrix like this:

	Low Impact	Medium Impact	High Impact	Critical Impact
Low Likelihood	Low	Low	Medium	Medium
Medium Likelihood	Low	Medium	High	High
High Likelihood	Medium	High	High	Critical

Your goal? Stay out of the red zone. Or as we call it:

The Oh-No-No Quadrant™.

How to Actually Perform an Analysis

Identify the Asset

E.g., Customer database, payment system, HR records.

Identify Threats & Vulnerabilities

Phishing, misconfigurations, ransomware, etc.

Evaluate Likelihood

Ask: "How likely is this threat to happen here, given our setup?"

Evaluate Impact

Ask: "If it did happen, what would the fallout look like?"

Map It on the Matrix

Place it in the grid and assign a risk level (Low, Medium, High, Critical)

Decide What to Do

Accept, avoid, transfer, or mitigate the risk. (That's in the next chapter)

Example Scenario: Phishing Attack

Let's say:

- **Asset:** Employee credentials
- **Threat:** Phishing email
- **Likelihood:** High (we get tons of them, users are clicky)
- **Impact:** Medium (could lead to internal access)

→ **Risk Rating: High**

You'd probably prioritize training, email filtering, and maybe even upgrading to phishing-resistant MFA (hint: do it).

Pro Tips for Better Analysis

- Use historical data from your logs, SIEM, or industry reports.
- Don't just guess — survey your SMEs (subject matter experts), even if they scare you.
- Consider control effectiveness — your firewall might be there, but is it working as intended or just... glowing quietly in the rack?
- Reassess regularly — the risk landscape changes faster than a TikTok trend.

Final Thoughts: It's Not Guesswork... It's Educated Guesswork

Look, nobody has a crystal ball. (Except maybe that weird guy in IT who smells like patch cables)

But with impact and likelihood analysis, you're not just reacting — you're proactively prioritizing. That's what makes a mature cyber risk program.

So go forth, measure your risks, map your chaos, and remember:

"You can't protect everything — but you can protect what matters most."

...Also, don't ignore those low-likelihood/high-impact scenarios.

Because those are the ones that show up in headlines.

3.3 Risk Scoring Models (CVSS, FAIR, Risk Matrices)

Cybersecurity risk scoring is like Tinder for threats — swipe right on the ones that'll ruin your life.

But seriously, without a scoring system, all risks kind of look the same: "bad". What we really need is a way to sort the truly hair-raising from the mildly annoying.

That's where risk scoring models come in. They help you answer:

- "What should we fix first?"
- "How bad is this really?"
- "Do we panic now or after lunch?"

Let's break down the big three players: CVSS, FAIR, and the good ol' Risk Matrix.

1. CVSS (Common Vulnerability Scoring System)

The rockstar of vuln scoring. CVSS is used globally to assess how severe a vulnerability is. Maintained by FIRST.org (not a superhero team, but close).

It's basically Yelp for vulnerabilities — but instead of stars, you get scores from 0.0 (meh) to 10.0 (code red).

CVSS Score Breakdown (v3.1):

CVSS splits into three metric groups:

- Base (constant factors)
- Attack Vector (network? physical?)
- Attack Complexity (low or high?)
- Privileges Required
- User Interaction
- Confidentiality / Integrity / Availability impact

Temporal (time-based)

- Is it being exploited in the wild?
- Is there a patch?
- Is the info reliable?

Environmental (custom to your org)

- Adjusts score based on your context (e.g., critical asset vs sandbox system)

Example:

Remote code execution on an internet-facing system, no user interaction, full system access.

→ CVSS Score: 9.8

That's a "drop everything and fix this now" situation.

Pros:

- Standardized & widely adopted
- Integrates with many tools (vuln scanners, SIEM, etc.)
- Makes patching decisions clearer

Cons:

- Only scores vulnerabilities, not entire risks
- Doesn't account for business impact (a 9.0 on a printer ≠ 9.0 on your production DB)

2. FAIR (Factor Analysis of Information Risk)

FAIR is like the philosopher of risk models. It's complex, deep, and tries to quantify actual financial loss.

Unlike CVSS, FAIR doesn't score just vulnerabilities — it evaluates the entire risk using solid math and Monte Carlo simulations (aka nerd magic).

Core Concepts:

Loss Event Frequency (how often does this happen?)

- Threat Event Frequency × Vulnerability

Probable Loss Magnitude (how bad is it?)

- **Primary loss:** direct costs (e.g. ransom, downtime)
- **Secondary loss:** reputation, legal, PR, etc.

Risk = Frequency × Magnitude

Output:

- You don't get "low, medium, high"
- You get things like:

"There's a 90% chance this risk costs us between $250k and $750k annually."

Pros:

- Very detailed and financially grounded
- Excellent for board-level reporting
- Works for any type of risk (not just IT)

Cons:

- Time- and resource-intensive
- Requires training (you don't just "wing" FAIR)
- Less ideal for quick decisions

Use FAIR when you want to speak CFO and justify investments in serious terms.

3. Risk Matrices

Ah, the humble Risk Matrix — the Swiss Army Knife of risk scoring.

This is what most orgs start with. You rate risks based on Likelihood and Impact, usually using qualitative labels:

	Low Impact	Medium Impact	High Impact	Critical Impact
Low Likelihood	Low	Low	Medium	Medium
Medium Likelihood	Low	Medium	High	High
High Likelihood	Medium	High	High	Critical

You just plop risks on the grid and prioritize the red ones first.

Pros:

- Easy to understand and quick to use
- Good for workshops, brainstorming, exec summaries
- Doesn't require fancy tools

Cons:

- Can be too subjective
- Can oversimplify risk
- Doesn't account for monetary value or external factors

Still, it's a fan favorite because it works for broad-level risk awareness without a PhD in cyber calculus.

Example: Let's Score a Risk 3 Ways

Scenario: There's a vulnerability in your HR portal that could leak employee data.

CVSS:

Score: 8.2 (High)

Action: Patch ASAP, high-priority vuln

FAIR:

- Estimated annual loss: $500k from lawsuits, fines, downtime
- Probability of loss this year: 25%
- Action: Cost-justify upgrading the web app and monitoring

Risk Matrix:

- **Likelihood:** Medium (only accessible to insiders)
- **Impact:** High (personal data breach)
- **Risk Rating:** High
- **Action:** Escalate to IT and Compliance

As you can see — each model offers a different lens. Together? They give a 360° view of the risk.

Quick Comparison Table

Model	Type	Output	Best For	Complexity
CVSS	Vulnerability scoring	0.0–10.0 score	Patch prioritization	Low
FAIR	Quantitative	Probable financial loss	Strategic risk investment	High
Risk Matrix	Qualitative	Low/Med/High/Critical	Everyday risk ranking	Medium

Final Thoughts: Risk Isn't Scary If You Can Score It

Scoring models are like cheat codes for risk management — they help you cut through the noise and focus on what actually matters. Whether you're a numbers person, a boardroom explainer, or just someone trying to keep the lights on without getting hacked — there's a model that fits.

Just remember:

"If everything is high risk, then nothing is."

So pick your tool, score wisely, and try not to cry when the FAIR model tells you that one overlooked control might cost you $3 million.

3.4 Business Impact Analysis (BIA)

"It's just a minor outage... until payroll stops running."

Let's face it: not every IT disaster is created equal. Your fancy digital signage going offline? Meh. Your ERP system that handles customer orders and billing? RED ALERT.

That's why we need Business Impact Analysis (BIA). It's the no-nonsense, "what happens if this goes down?" exercise that separates mission-critical systems from the nice-to-haves.

BIA is like prepping for a zombie apocalypse :

- What can we live without?
- What do we absolutely need to survive?
- How long before it's game over?

Let's break it down.

What Is a Business Impact Analysis?

BIA is the process of identifying the critical business functions and evaluating the consequences of their disruption.

In plain speak:

"If this system crashes, what's the damage — and how fast do we need it back?"

It's not just a cybersecurity exercise. It ties directly into:

- Disaster recovery (DR)
- Business continuity planning (BCP)
- Risk prioritization
- Resource allocation

Key Objectives of a BIA

Identify Essential Processes

What keeps the business running day-to-day?

Understand Dependencies

Systems, people, applications, third-party vendors — what's holding things together?

Estimate Downtime Impact

Financial loss, reputational hit, regulatory pain, etc.

Define Recovery Priorities

What needs to be up in 2 hours vs 2 weeks?

Core Components of a BIA

Let's go through the big hitters in a typical BIA:

1. Recovery Time Objective (RTO)

"How soon must this be back online?"

This is your acceptable downtime — the max time a process can be unavailable without causing significant harm.

Example:

- Payroll system RTO = 48 hours (you've got a buffer before HR starts a mutiny)

2. Recovery Point Objective (RPO)

"How much data can we afford to lose?"

This defines the maximum tolerable data loss, usually in hours or minutes.

Example:

- **RPO = 4 hours** → You can lose up to 4 hours of data without major issues (better hope those backups are running)

3. Impact Types to Measure:

- **Financial** (lost revenue, fines, penalties)
- **Reputational** (customer churn, media fallout)
- **Operational** (process delays, productivity loss)
- **Legal/Regulatory** (compliance violations)
- **Health & Safety** (for OT/ICS/healthcare sectors)

4. Impact Severity Levels:

Use a scale like:

- **Low:** Minor inconvenience
- **Medium:** Moderate disruption
- **High:** Severe impact on operations

- **Critical:** Show-stopping catastrophe

Example Table: BIA Summary for Key Business Functions

Business Function	System	RTO	RPO	Impact if Down	Priority
Payroll	HRMS	48h	24h	Financial + Legal	High
E-commerce	Website	2h	15m	Revenue loss	Critical
Marketing	CMS	5d	48h	Low productivity	Low
Customer Support	CRM	8h	4h	Reputational	Medium

Yep, that's right — marketing can wait a bit. Sorry, folks

Who Should Be Involved in a BIA?

- **Department Heads** – They know what breaks the business
- **IT/Infosec** – Understand system dependencies and risks
- **Finance** – Help quantify monetary impact
- **Legal & Compliance** – Understand regulatory requirements
- **Operations** – Know how long the business can run on fumes

BIA is not just for the IT team locked in a basement — it's a full-on team sport.

Common Pitfalls to Avoid

Treating everything as "critical"

If everything is high-priority, nothing is.

Skipping non-technical impacts

Reputation, legal exposure, and even employee morale matter.

Ignoring dependencies

Your "critical" app might rely on three "non-critical" systems. Oops.

One-and-done mindset

BIA is a living process — update it as the business grows, changes, or merges with a snack food company for some reason.

Pro Tips

Map systems to business processes

→ It's not just about servers, it's about what they do for the business.

Align with DR/BCP planning

→ BIA is the foundation for those.

Use real incidents to validate

→ Remember that one time payroll went down? Let's not do that again.

Visualize results

→ Heatmaps, charts, or tiered recovery groups help you explain to leadership why marketing's cat meme server isn't getting top priority.

Real-Life Scenario: Zombie Outbreak (Okay, Not Really)

Let's say there's a ransomware attack that takes down:

- Your CRM
- Internal email
- Payroll system

Here's how BIA helps:

- **CRM:** Reputational + revenue → Restore within 8 hours
- **Email:** Annoying, but Slack is still up → Medium priority
- **Payroll:** Restore in 2 days max or face regulatory trouble

Without a BIA? You'd be rebooting the coffee machine first because it's "on the list"

Final Thoughts: BIA is Boring... Until It Saves Your Bacon

Look, we get it. Business Impact Analysis doesn't sound sexy. But when disaster strikes, BIA is the thing that keeps your company from turning into chaos stew.

It's the blueprint for:

- What to recover first
- Who gets the emergency calls
- How much pain you're willing to tolerate

So next time someone says, "It's just a server," remind them:

"Yeah, and it's the one that processes $2M/day in orders."

3.5 Prioritization Techniques and Decision Trees

"*When everything's on fire, put out the one near the gas tank first.*"

Welcome to the part of risk management where we stop staring at problems and actually start doing something about them — smartly, methodically, and without setting our hair on fire (ideally).

You've got your risk scores, your business impact data, and your budget spreadsheet that says "lol no" in all caps. So how do you prioritize what to tackle first?

Let me introduce you to a few friends:

- Risk Prioritization Techniques
- Decision Trees

They're like GPS for cyber chaos: helping you make better, faster decisions under pressure and resource constraints.

Why Prioritize?

Because doing everything is impossible, and doing nothing is a career-ending move.

Risk prioritization helps answer:

- Which risks do we mitigate now?
- Which do we monitor?
- Which do we accept and pray about?

Prioritization Techniques

Let's break down a few of the most common and practical methods to rank those pesky cyber risks.

1. Risk Matrix (Revisited)

Remember our good friend from earlier? A simple likelihood vs impact heatmap.

	Low Impact	Medium Impact	High Impact	Critical Impact
Low Likelihood	Low	Low	Medium	Medium
Medium Likelihood	Low	Medium	High	High
High Likelihood	Medium	High	High	Critical

The redder the cell, the higher the priority.

Best For: Fast triage

Watch Out For: Oversimplification, too much subjectivity

2. Weighted Scoring

If you're the kind of person who likes spreadsheets and fairness, this one's for you.

Assign weights to criteria like:

- **Exploitability** (25%)
- **Business Impact** (35%)
- **Recovery Cost** (20%)
- **Legal Consequences** (20%)

Then rate each risk, multiply, and boom — you've got a score!

Example:

Risk	Exploitability (25%)	Impact (35%)	Cost (20%)	Legal (20%)	Total Score
Phishing Emails	4	3	2	2	3.05
Unpatched DB Vuln	5	5	4	5	4.7

The higher the score, the higher the priority.

Best For: Nuanced, multi-factor analysis

Watch Out For: Overcomplicating things — don't score yourself into paralysis

3. Pareto Principle (80/20 Rule)

Focus on the 20% of risks that cause 80% of your potential pain.

Instead of boiling the ocean, look for:

- The most common attack paths
- The top vulnerabilities being actively exploited
- The loudest logs in your SIEM

Best For: Quick wins, resource-strapped teams

Watch Out For: Neglecting low-frequency but high-impact risks

4. Risk Appetite Filtering

Sometimes you don't prioritize based on score — you prioritize based on whether it exceeds your organization's risk appetite.

Anything above your "unacceptable" threshold gets fast-tracked

Anything below it might be accepted, deferred, or insured

Think of it as a digital red line — once crossed, it's go-time.

Enter the Decision Tree: Cybersecurity's "Choose Your Own Adventure"

You remember those books where you'd turn to page 27 to slay the dragon or page 43 to get eaten by a troll? Well, that's basically what a Decision Tree is — but with fewer trolls and more business continuity.

What Is a Decision Tree?

A visual branching tool that maps out "if this, then that" choices to guide decision-making.

Great for:

- Incident response
- Patch management
- Vendor risk evaluation
- Risk treatment planning

Basic Decision Tree Flow

Here's a simplified version of a risk decision tree for vulnerabilities:

Is the system internet-facing?

├── *Yes*

│ └── *Is the vulnerability critical?*

│ ├── *Yes → Patch immediately*

│ └── *No → Schedule patch*

└── *No*

└── *Is it exploitable internally?*

├── *Yes → Patch in next cycle*

└── *No → Monitor only*

Simple, right? But extremely useful under pressure when you're drowning in alerts and need clarity, fast.

Real-Life Use Case: Third-Party Vendor Risk

Does vendor process customer data?

├── *Yes*

│ └── *Are they SOC2 or ISO 27001 certified?*

│ ├── *Yes → Proceed with regular contract*

│ └── *No → Require additional due diligence*

└── *No*

└── *Low priority — monitor annually*

This saves hours of meetings and emails. Seriously.

Putting It All Together

Let's say you've got 25 risks logged in your risk register. What now?

1. Use weighted scoring to rank top threats
2. Apply the Pareto Principle to find quick wins
3. Cross-check against risk appetite
4. Use a decision tree for treatment decisions
5. Plot high scorers into your risk matrix to visualize urgency

It's not just about being methodical. It's about being consistently rational — especially when the panic button's flashing.

Bonus Tip: Prioritization ≠ Procrastination

Just because something's low-priority doesn't mean you never handle it. It just means:

- You handle higher-impact stuff first
- You might accept the risk
- Or find a low-effort mitigation (e.g., disabling unused services)

Don't use prioritization as an excuse to do nothing. It's not a security strategy — it's a sorting strategy.

Final Thoughts: Triage Now, Nap Later

Prioritization is the thing that helps your team:

- Focus
- Communicate
- Defend

And stay sane while the threat landscape goes full Jumanji on you

So build your risk heatmaps. Score your threats. Draw those trees. And most importantly — don't let indecision be your biggest vulnerability.

"If everything is a priority... nothing gets done. Except stress."

Chapter 4: Risk Mitigation Strategies

So you've got threats coming from every corner of the digital jungle, and your firewall is holding the line like a lone cowboy at high noon. Time to upgrade your defenses! Whether it's a fancy intrusion detection system or just finally forcing Bob from accounting to use two-factor authentication, mitigation is where we turn chaos into calm.

This chapter outlines the various strategies and tools available to reduce or eliminate cyber risk. You'll learn about defense-in-depth architectures, categories of security controls (technical, administrative, and physical), and contemporary paradigms like Zero Trust and Security by Design. These practices form the bedrock of proactive cybersecurity risk management.

4.1 Defense-in-Depth Architecture

"One firewall to rule them all"? Yeah... that's how the bad guys win.

Let's be real: relying on a single security control is like locking your front door but leaving all the windows open and a ladder in the backyard.

That's why we roll with Defense-in-Depth (DiD) — a layered, strategic approach to cybersecurity that ensures if one layer fails, another one's ready to catch the breach (like a digital safety net).

You wouldn't wear a single sock to a snowstorm, right? Let's stack those layers, friend.

What is Defense-in-Depth?

Defense-in-Depth is a security strategy that uses multiple layers of defense across the network, systems, applications, and people to protect data and assets.

Think of it like a medieval castle:

- **Moat** = Network firewall
- **Outer wall** = Intrusion detection systems
- **Guards** = Endpoint protection
- **Inner sanctum** = Encrypted data vault

If one layer fails, the attacker still has a bad day ahead.

Goals of Defense-in-Depth

- Delay attackers long enough to detect and respond
- Reduce single points of failure
- Protect assets even if one control is bypassed
- Support business continuity (because security without uptime is just expensive paranoia)

Key Layers of a Defense-in-Depth Strategy

Let's break down the main layers like a delicious security burrito:

1. Physical Security

Let's not forget the basics:

- Locked server rooms

- Security cameras
- Badge access
- Alarms

Because if someone can just walk out with your server, all that fancy encryption won't mean squat.

Tip: Don't laugh — someone once got hacked because their data center door lock was held open by a folded coffee cup.

2. Perimeter Security

The outer boundary of your network — your first digital line of defense:

- Firewalls
- Border routers with ACLs
- DDoS protection

But here's the catch: there is no traditional perimeter anymore thanks to cloud, remote work, and BYOD. So this layer matters, but it ain't enough.

3. Network Security

Once inside the "walls," attackers can move laterally... unless you make life hard:

- VLANs and segmentation
- Internal firewalls
- IDS/IPS (Intrusion Detection/Prevention Systems)
- Network access control (NAC)
- Isolation = containment = less chaos when things go boom

4. Endpoint Security

Every laptop, desktop, and mobile device is a front line:

- Anti-malware
- EDR (Endpoint Detection & Response)
- Disk encryption
- USB port restrictions (because some people still plug in found flash drives)

5. Application Security

Applications are juicy targets, especially web apps:

- Secure coding practices
- WAFs (Web Application Firewalls)
- Regular testing: SAST, DAST, IAST, etc.
- Patch. Your. Stuff. Seriously.

6. Data Security

Because at the end of the day, data is the prize:

- Encryption at rest and in transit
- Access controls (RBAC/ABAC)
- Data loss prevention (DLP)
- Backups and secure storage

Bonus tip: Backups are useless if you don't test them. Don't be that person.

7. Identity & Access Management (IAM)

Your systems are only as secure as who's allowed in:

- MFA (Multi-Factor Authentication)
- Least privilege access
- Identity federation & SSO
- Role reviews & access recertification

Hackers don't always break in — sometimes, they just log in.

8. Security Monitoring & Incident Response

You can't defend what you can't see:

- SIEM tools
- Log analysis
- Threat hunting
- SOC (Security Operations Center)

Detect fast. Respond faster. And never assume you're not a target.

9. User Awareness & Training

The human firewall is either your strongest layer... or your biggest vulnerability:

- Phishing simulations
- Security awareness training
- Clear policies and acceptable use guidelines

Let's be honest: if Dave from accounting keeps clicking "Download Invoice.exe," your EDR better be on point.

Example: Layered Defense in Action

Say a hacker sends a phishing email with a malicious link. Here's how DiD saves your bacon:

- **Email** gateway blocks known bad attachments
- **Firewall** blocks access to shady IPs
- **Endpoint** AV detects and quarantines the payload
- **EDR** flags unusual behavior on the device
- **SIEM** sends an alert to the SOC
- **User** training helps the recipient report the email

Any one of those could fail — but all together? Chef's kiss.

Challenges with DiD

It's not all roses and packet filters:

- **Cost:** More tools = more $$$
- **Complexity:** Layers add management overhead
- **Integration:** Tools must work together, not against each other
- **Complacency:** "We have 6 tools, so we're safe" ← famous last words

Bonus: Cloud & Defense-in-Depth

With cloud and hybrid environments, DiD takes on a new flavor:

- Use cloud-native firewalls & IAM
- Secure APIs and storage buckets
- Monitor configs via CSPM tools
- Don't forget container security

Yes, even your serverless functions need protection.

Final Thoughts: Security Like Shrek (Yep, That's Right)

Just like ogres and onions, security has layers.

If someone peels through one layer, you want more waiting underneath. That's Defense-in-Depth: not paranoid, just prepared.

So next time someone asks, "Can't we just install a firewall and call it a day?" — gently hand them this chapter... then quietly take their admin rights.

4.2 Security Controls (Administrative, Technical, Physical)

> **Security controls are like layers of cake** — some are sweet, some are dense, and some are just for decoration... but all of them matter if you want to stay protected (and not poisoned)."

Cybersecurity isn't just about locking down your network — it's about implementing the right controls in the right places. That means combining people, processes, and tech like a three-headed security dragon.

In this chapter, we're going to break security controls into three main categories:

- Administrative
- Technical
- Physical

Together, they form the holy trinity of protection — like peanut butter, jelly, and a baseball bat under the desk (just in case).

What Are Security Controls?

Security controls are safeguards or countermeasures designed to:

- Reduce risk
- Detect threats
- Protect assets
- Ensure compliance
- Make attackers cry

They can be preventive, detective, or corrective, depending on the goal:

- **Preventive:** Stop stuff before it happens (e.g. access control)
- **Detective:** Find out when it does happen (e.g. audit logs)
- **Corrective:** Fix the damage and recover (e.g. backup restoration)

1. Administrative Controls

"Policies and paperwork... aka the things everyone agrees to and no one reads."

These are the people and policy-based controls that govern how your organization operates securely.

Examples:

- Security policies (e.g. Acceptable Use Policy)
- Access control policies
- Risk assessments
- Training and awareness programs
- Vendor and third-party management
- Incident response plans
- Change management procedures

Think of administrative controls as the rules of the game. They set the expectations and give your team a roadmap for secure behavior.

Why They Matter:

You can have the best tech in the world, but if people aren't following processes (or don't even know they exist), it's like installing a top-notch alarm system and leaving the door wide open.

Real talk: If Dave from Sales reuses his "Password123" login across your payroll system, no amount of firewalls will save you.

2. Technical Controls

"The shiny stuff the IT team drools over — with logs, alerts, and occasional cursing."

Technical (or logical) controls are the technology-based solutions that enforce your security policies.

Examples:

- Firewalls (network or host-based)
- Encryption (data at rest and in transit)
- Antivirus & anti-malware
- Multi-factor authentication (MFA)
- Intrusion detection/prevention systems (IDS/IPS)
- Access control lists (ACLs)
- SIEM systems
- Vulnerability scanners
- Data loss prevention (DLP)

These are your hands-on, button-clicking, alert-flashing defenses. They can often respond faster than humans and are essential for scaling security across complex environments.

Why They Matter:

Technology can help you enforce policies consistently and react in milliseconds to threats humans might miss. Plus, no one forgets to apply a firewall rule... unless they're asleep at the console (which, let's face it, sometimes happens).

3. Physical Controls

"Because your cybersecurity plan should include locking the door to the server room."

Physical controls protect the actual buildings, devices, and infrastructure that house your digital assets.

Examples:

- Security guards
- Badge access systems
- Locked doors and server cages
- CCTV surveillance
- Fences, gates, and bollards (yes, even parking lot defenses count)
- Environmental controls (fire suppression, HVAC, water sensors)
- Visitor logs & escort policies

Why They Matter:

Cyber attacks don't always start in cyberspace. Someone walking into your data center and yanking out a hard drive can bypass every digital defense you've got.

True story: A data breach once happened because a cleaning crew found an unsecured laptop and took it home to play solitaire. Not even kidding.

Putting It All Together: The Security Control Sandwich

Let's say you're trying to protect sensitive customer data in your CRM system. Here's what the three types of controls might look like:

Control Type	Example
Administrative	Data classification policy, training staff
Technical	Role-based access, encryption, DLP
Physical	Locked server room, biometric access, CCTV

Each layer complements the others. If one fails, the others back it up. You want redundancy, not wishful thinking.

Bonus: Mapping Controls to Risk

When performing risk management, every identified risk should map to at least one control in each of the three categories.

- **Example:** Risk = "Unauthorized access to payroll data"
- **Admin:** Policy says only HR can access payroll
- **Technical:** RBAC + MFA on payroll app
- **Physical:** Server room is locked; logs are kept of who enters

This approach satisfies auditors, secures data, and makes your CISO sleep a little easier at night.

Framework Tie-In: Where They Fit

You'll see this classification used in frameworks like:

- **NIST SP 800-53** (maps hundreds of controls into these categories)
- **ISO/IEC 27001** (Annex A control families)
- CIS Controls
- **PCI DSS** (especially for access, data, and facility controls)

So yeah... knowing your control types isn't just a trivia flex — it's mandatory for compliance.

Final Thoughts: Don't Just Throw Tools at the Problem

Too many orgs think buying a new tool = being secure. But without proper policies and physical protection, that's like buying a lock and never using it.

Your cyber defense should be layered, balanced, and always mapped to the real-world threats you face.

"Think of your controls like your morning routine: *brushing your teeth is great (technical), remembering to do it is important (administrative), and keeping your toothbrush in a clean bathroom? That's physical."*

4.3 Security by Design & Zero Trust Principles

"If your system wasn't designed to be secure from the start... it's basically a beautiful house with no locks and a welcome mat that says: 'Hack me, I dare you.'"

Let's face it — patching up a system after it's been hacked is like trying to weld armor onto a car while you're driving it into battle.

That's why Security by Design and Zero Trust have become the Batman and Robin of modern cybersecurity: proactive, paranoid (in a good way), and ready to wreck cybercriminals' day.

What is Security by Design?

Security by Design (SbD) means building security into every stage of a system's lifecycle — from architecture and design to development, deployment, and even decommissioning.

Rather than bolting on security at the end (when everything's already duct-taped together), SbD ensures it's woven into the very DNA of your tech stack.

Core Ideas:

- Security is not a feature — it's a foundation
- Threat modeling starts on day one
- Secure coding practices are mandatory
- Privacy and compliance are baked in, not sprinkled on
- Everyone — not just security pros — shares responsibility

Fun analogy: You wouldn't build a submarine and then wonder if it's waterproof, right?

Principles of Security by Design

Here's how SbD stays ahead of the curve (and attackers):

1. Least Privilege Access

Every user and service gets only the permissions they absolutely need — and nothing more. No more "just in case" admin access for Bob from Marketing.

2. Fail Securely

If something breaks, it should break in a way that doesn't expose data or functionality. That means error messages shouldn't be mini-novels explaining your entire server stack.

3. Secure Defaults

Default settings should prioritize security, not convenience. Disable open ports, turn off unused services, and make strong passwords the rule — not the optional checkbox.

4. Defense in Depth (again!)

Layers of controls ensure one failure doesn't mean total compromise. If attackers breach one layer, they hit a second — then a third.

5. Keep It Simple (KISS)

Complexity is the enemy of security. The more convoluted your system, the more room there is for bugs, misconfigs, and whoopsies.

What is Zero Trust?

Zero Trust takes Security by Design and gives it an attitude. It's a modern security model based on one ruthless belief:

"Never trust. Always verify."

No device, user, or app is automatically trusted — not even the CEO's iPad. Whether you're inside the network or connecting remotely from the café Wi-Fi, everything must be authenticated, authorized, and continuously validated.

Basically, Zero Trust assumes the bad guys are already in your network. So instead of building walls and hoping for the best, you limit blast radius, enforce tight controls, and inspect everything.

Pillars of Zero Trust

Let's break down what makes Zero Trust tick:

1. Identity Verification Everywhere

- **Strong authentication** (like MFA)
- **Contextual access** (location, device health, time of day)
- **Continuous monitoring** (not just login — after too)

2. Device Trustworthiness

- Endpoint health checks
- Up-to-date patches and AV
- Only allow access from compliant devices

3. Least Privilege Access (again!)

- Just-in-time (JIT) access
- Role-based access control (RBAC)
- Time-based access windows

4. Micro-Segmentation

- Isolate resources into tiny trust zones
- Prevent lateral movement inside the network
- Stop attackers from roaming around like it's an open buffet

5. Visibility and Analytics

- Log everything
- Use behavior analytics and anomaly detection
- Centralize insights with a SIEM or XDR platform

Zero Trust doesn't mean "no trust ever" — it means trust is earned, verified, and revoked if suspicious.

Zero Trust vs. Traditional Security

Traditional Model	Zero Trust Model
Perimeter-based ("trusted inside")	No implicit trust anywhere
One-time authentication	Continuous verification
Broad access based on role	Granular access, often temporary
Flat networks	Micro-segmented environments
Reactive	Proactive and adaptive

SbD + Zero Trust in the Cloud

Perfect match! Cloud environments actually thrive under these principles:

- Use IAM policies to restrict access to specific APIs
- Leverage cloud-native firewalls and service perimeters
- Implement serverless zero trust by default
- Use automation to revoke unused access keys or detect anomalies

Your cloud setup shouldn't rely on old castle-and-moat models. Instead, it should look like Fort Knox inside every single container.

Real-World Example: Applying SbD + Zero Trust

Let's say you're building a customer portal.

With Security by Design:

- You define roles & access before coding begins
- You use secure libraries and sanitize input from day one
- You encrypt all customer data and log every login attempt

With Zero Trust:

- Users must use MFA
- Access is scoped by role and expires after X hours
- All traffic is encrypted, even internal service-to-service calls
- If Bob logs in from a new device in a new country — boom, anomaly detected, access flagged

This kind of proactive setup stops breaches before they happen, and limits the damage if they do.

Challenges to Expect

- **Complex integration:** Implementing Zero Trust across legacy systems? That's a therapy session waiting to happen.
- **Culture shift:** People hate more logins and restrictions — especially executives.
- **Cost:** Identity management, analytics, and segmentation tools can add up.
- **Fatigue:** Alert fatigue, MFA fatigue, and policy fatigue are real. Balance is key.

Final Thoughts: Trust Issues (In a Good Way)

Security by Design + Zero Trust isn't just a tech upgrade — it's a mindset. You're not building your house in a nice neighborhood anymore. You're building it in a cyberpunk dystopia where every neighbor is a hacker.

So build smart. Validate everything. Trust no one (not even your toaster).

Because if "trust but verify" was the old way... the new way is just: "verify, monitor, restrict, repeat."

4.4 Patch Management and Secure Configuration

"If systems were superheroes, unpatched software would be the one wearing a cape made of tissue paper and yelling, 'I'm invincible!' — right before getting hacked."

Security isn't just about stopping attackers — it's about not leaving the front door open in the first place. That's where patch management and secure configuration come into play. These two are often overlooked, wildly underappreciated, and absolutely essential.

Let's break down what they are, why they matter, and how not doing them turns your network into a buffet for threat actors.

What Is Patch Management?

Patch Management is the process of identifying, acquiring, testing, and deploying software updates — also known as patches — to fix security vulnerabilities and bugs.

Patches don't just fix typos in the UI. They often:

- Close security holes
- Improve performance
- Add new security features
- Prevent attackers from exploiting known flaws

Wanna know how attackers get in? They read patch notes... and target everyone who hasn't updated yet.

Real-World Example:

WannaCry exploited a vulnerability in Windows that Microsoft had already patched. But orgs who hadn't applied it? Boom — ransomware spread like a virus at a kindergarten birthday party.

Patch Management Process (The Not-Boring Version)

Here's a simplified, real-human process:

Inventory Your Assets

Know what hardware, OSes, and apps are running. You can't patch what you don't know exists (surprise, old forgotten server in the closet).

Monitor for Updates

Subscribe to vendor bulletins (Microsoft, Adobe, etc.), use vulnerability feeds (like NVD), or tools like WSUS, SCCM, or third-party patch managers.

Evaluate Risk

Not every patch is equal. Prioritize critical security updates, especially those with CVEs and known exploits in the wild.

Test Before You Wreck

Apply patches in a test environment first. Nothing says "fun Friday" like crashing production with a botched patch.

Deploy Strategically

Roll out in phases if possible, track progress, and avoid patching your entire infrastructure during lunch breaks or holidays.

Verify and Log It

Confirm the patch was successfully installed, and keep records for compliance and incident response.

Rinse, Repeat, Forever

Patch management is like laundry — it never ends, but skipping it starts to smell real fast.

What Is Secure Configuration?

Secure configuration means setting up systems, software, and devices in a way that minimizes risk — right out of the box.

Here's the twist: most default settings are designed for ease of use, not security.

That's like buying a house and leaving all the windows open because "the breeze feels nice."

Common Default Risks:

- Default passwords (admin/admin, anyone?)
- Unused open ports/services
- Excessive user permissions
- Unencrypted communication
- Logging disabled

Secure Configuration Best Practices

1. Change Default Credentials

Yes, even your smart fridge and router. Attackers scan the internet specifically for devices with factory logins.

2. Disable Unused Services

If you don't use FTP, RDP, Telnet — turn it off. Fewer doors = fewer ways in.

3. Harden OS and Applications

Apply benchmarks from sources like:

- CIS Benchmarks (gold standard)
- DISA STIGs
- Vendor hardening guides

These guides are basically security cheat codes for every OS, DB, browser, and toaster running Wi-Fi.

4. Principle of Least Functionality

Only install what's necessary. You don't need 17 apps on your server "just in case."

5. Continuous Monitoring

Regularly scan your configs using tools like:

- SCAP scanners
- OpenSCAP
- Chef InSpec
- Ansible with audit modules

Patch vs. Config: What's the Difference?

Feature	Patch Management	Secure Configuration
Purpose	Fix known vulnerabilities	Prevent misconfigurations
Frequency	Ongoing (monthly, weekly)	Once + monitored/updated
Tools Used	WSUS, SCCM, PDQ, etc.	CIS-CAT, InSpec, Ansible
Focus	Vendor updates	Internal security posture
Risk of Skipping	Known exploits	Easy attack vectors

Both are essential for a strong security foundation, and skipping either is like choosing between locking your front door OR closing your windows.

Cloud & Containers: Don't Forget Me!

In cloud and containerized environments:

- Use hardened base images (Amazon, Ubuntu, Red Hat all offer them)
- Automate patching pipelines with CI/CD integration
- Apply infrastructure-as-code scanning tools (like Terraform + tfsec)
- Monitor container registries for vulnerable dependencies

Your EC2, Lambda, or Kubernetes pod still needs patching and proper config. Cloud ≠ magic security shield.

Automation is Your Friend

Manual patching and config hardening is like knitting sweaters for a stadium of penguins — noble, but painfully slow.

Use tools like:

- **Ansible, Puppet, Chef** (for config management)
- **Qualys, Rapid7, Tenable** (for vulnerability/patch scanning)
- **AWS Systems Manager Patch Manager** (for EC2 fleets)
- **Microsoft Intune** (for endpoint control)

Automate what you can, log what you must, and always know what's going on under the hood.

Final Thoughts: Update or Get Owned

Unpatched systems and bad configs are #1 and #2 on the "Top 10 ways to get hacked" list. Right ahead of "clicking suspicious links" and "naming your password 'password.'"

"Patch often. Configure wisely. And never trust a system with an uptime of 3 years — that means no one's touched it in 3 years... including to secure it."

4.5 Security Awareness and Human Factor Defense

"Your firewall can be Fort Knox, your encryption can rival the CIA, but it only takes one employee clicking 'Open Attachment' on a sketchy email from 'Prince_Nigeria_Official' to bring the whole thing down."

Welcome to the human side of cybersecurity — where logic meets emotion, and common sense takes a lunch break. Let's talk about the biggest vulnerability in your network: people.

Yup, humans. Friendly, well-meaning, occasionally distracted humans. You can have all the latest tools and tech, but if your staff thinks phishing is a sport, you're in trouble.

Why Security Awareness Matters

You can't patch people. (If only there was a monthly update for that, right?)

Technology handles a lot of heavy lifting — but attackers don't always go after firewalls. They go after Karen in Accounting with a well-crafted email and a link that totally looks like the company's payroll login.

Cybersecurity isn't just IT's job anymore. It's everyone's job. From the intern to the CEO, everyone has a digital footprint — and attackers know how to exploit the weakest link.

Human Error by the Numbers

Let's throw some spicy stats at you:

- 95% of cybersecurity breaches are caused by human error – IBM
- Phishing accounts for 36% of all breaches – Verizon DBIR
- Over 20% of employees will click on a phishing email. Of those, 50% will enter credentials

The takeaway? Training people can't be optional. It's the backbone of your cyber defense.

What is Security Awareness Training?

Security Awareness Training (SAT) is the process of educating users about cybersecurity risks, safe behaviors, and policies.

The goal isn't to turn everyone into hackers (though that'd be cool). It's to build a culture where security is second nature — like buckling your seatbelt.

Core Topics of a Great Training Program

Let's break down what you should be teaching:

1. Phishing & Social Engineering

- Recognize suspicious emails, texts, and calls

- Don't click links or download unknown attachments
- Don't give out sensitive info to "IT support" that sounds like they just woke up

2. Password Hygiene

- Use strong, unique passwords
- Enable MFA wherever possible
- Never write passwords on sticky notes... especially on your monitor

3. Data Handling & Classification

- Know what data is sensitive
- Store, share, and delete it securely
- Don't upload confidential data to random cloud drives

4. Device and Endpoint Security

- Lock your screen when you leave your desk
- Don't install unauthorized software
- Keep your devices updated

5. Remote Work Safety

- Use VPNs on public Wi-Fi (Starbucks isn't a secure location, sorry)
- Don't leave laptops in cars (unless you like data breaches with your coffee)
- Report lost or stolen devices immediately

6. Incident Reporting

- Don't panic — report!
- If you think something sketchy happened, notify IT/security fast
- Faster response = less damage

Fun (and Effective) Training Formats

Your awareness program doesn't have to be death-by-PowerPoint. Spice it up with:

- Simulated phishing tests (nothing wakes folks up like getting duped)
- Short, engaging training videos

- Interactive quizzes or games
- In-person or virtual workshops
- Guest speakers or hacker demos (yes, it's a thing, and yes, people love it)

The goal: make it stick. If they're laughing and learning, you're doing it right.

Building a Security-Conscious Culture

Security isn't just a "training day." It's a mindset — a culture. You want people to:

- Feel comfortable reporting mistakes (no shame zone!)
- Call out sketchy activity (even if it's from Bob in Sales)
- Take pride in being part of the defense team

Create security champions across departments — folks who get extra training and help their teams stay sharp.

Metrics That Matter

How do you know your training's working?

Track stuff like:

- % of users completing training
- Phishing test click rates (and how they improve)
- Incident report volume (higher = better awareness!)
- Password reset frequency (yes, it tells you something!)

If your phishing click rate drops from 25% to 2%, congratulations — your humans are learning not to fall for Nigerian princes and fake invoices.

Bonus Tip: Gamify It!

Who said security can't be fun?

Offer:

- Leaderboards for secure behaviors
- Prizes for top security quiz scorers
- Department-wide phishing challenges
- "Capture the Flag" mini games

People love games. And they remember lessons better when they're playing — not snoozing.

Common Roadblocks (And How to Fix Them)

"I don't have time for this."

Make training short, snappy, and accessible on-demand.

"This stuff is boring."

Use humor, storytelling, and real-world hacks to keep it lively.

"I already know all this."

Great, prove it! Simulations and quizzes will test that confidence.

"Security is IT's job."

That's like saying fire safety is just the fire department's job.

Final Thoughts: People Are the Perimeter

In the old days, we protected the network. Now? The network is everywhere — remote laptops, mobile phones, SaaS apps, smart toasters.

Your people are the new perimeter.

Train them. Empower them. And most importantly, don't underestimate them. Even Steve can learn to spot a phishing scam... eventually.

Chapter 5: Governance, Policy, and Compliance

Ah, policies—the part of cybersecurity that makes you feel like you're drowning in paperwork written by someone who has never actually used a computer. But trust us, this isn't just about boring rules. Governance and compliance are your digital seatbelts, helping you survive the legal rollercoaster when something hits the fan (and it will).

This chapter focuses on the organizational structures, policies, and compliance requirements that underpin a sound cybersecurity risk program. From international regulations like GDPR and HIPAA to internal governance models and audit practices, we examine how to ensure accountability, legal adherence, and ethical operations in the digital domain.

5.1 Cybersecurity Governance Models

> *"Because sometimes, shouting 'We need better security!' into the void isn't quite enough. You need structure, accountability... and maybe a few spreadsheets."*

Let's be honest — governance doesn't sound as thrilling as a high-speed ransomware takedown or catching a phishing scam in action. But here's the thing: without governance, all that cool tech stuff? It falls apart faster than a cheap USB stick.

Cybersecurity governance is how we make smart decisions, assign responsibility, and keep the entire security program aligned with business goals — not just IT goals.

What is Cybersecurity Governance?

In plain English, cybersecurity governance is the framework of rules, roles, and processes that ensure an organization's security strategy is consistent, well-managed, and in sync with its mission.

Think of it like this:

- **Cybersecurity** = the car
- **Governance** = the steering wheel + GPS

You can build the most high-tech vehicle in the world, but without direction and control, you're still gonna drive straight into a firewall (pun 100% intended).

Why Governance Matters

Let's paint a picture:

- Your security team installs next-gen firewalls
- Devs are pushing unvetted code to production
- Marketing is using free cloud tools without approval

Congrats! You're now the proud owner of a chaotic mess that no tool alone can fix.

Governance ensures that:

- Everyone follows the same rules
- Policies are enforced consistently
- Leadership has visibility and accountability
- Risk appetite is understood (Are we risk-tolerant? Risk-averse? Just plain risky?)

Key Elements of Cybersecurity Governance

Let's break down what actually goes into a solid governance model:

1. Policies and Standards

- These are your "laws of the land."
- Define what is and isn't acceptable behavior.
- Examples: Acceptable Use Policy, Password Policy, Data Handling Standards.

Pro tip: Don't just copy-paste templates. Make sure they reflect your organization's reality — and are actually enforceable.

2. Roles and Responsibilities

- **Who owns what?**
- **CISOs don't do it all alone** (even if we like pretending we do).

Common roles:

- **CISO:** Strategy, reporting to execs
- **IT Security Team:** Operations, defense
- **Risk Manager:** Aligning risks with business strategy
- **Business Units:** Front-line defenders (yes, even Bob in Sales)

Everyone plays a part — especially those clicking emails all day.

3. Risk Management Alignment

Governance isn't just about saying "no" — it's about understanding and managing cyber risk in a business context.

- Use risk frameworks (NIST RMF, FAIR, ISO 27005)
- Track and communicate risk to stakeholders
- Make decisions based on risk tolerance (Not every risk must be eliminated. Some can be accepted... like pineapple on pizza.)

4. Performance Measurement & KPIs

You can't manage what you don't measure.

Great governance includes:

- Metrics (e.g., # of incidents, % patched systems, training completion rates)

- Dashboards for execs who don't want to hear about TCP/IP but love pie charts
- Reviews to ensure policies are actually working

5. Continuous Improvement

Cyber threats evolve. So should your governance.

Set up:

- Annual policy reviews
- Post-incident lessons learned (because sometimes we need to admit, "Yeah, that didn't go well...")
- Maturity models (like CMMI or NIST CSF tiers) to level-up your program

Popular Cybersecurity Governance Models

Let's look at a few well-known frameworks and models that can help you build your governance foundation:

NIST Cybersecurity Framework (CSF)

- Functions: Identify, Protect, Detect, Respond, Recover
- Offers a structured way to align cybersecurity with business needs
- Very adaptable for different industries

Bonus: Executives love NIST CSF. It makes them feel like they "get" cybersecurity.

ISO/IEC 27001

- International standard for information security management systems (ISMS)
- Focuses on risk management, control implementation, and continuous improvement
- Heavy on documentation, but rock solid for compliance-driven environments

Pro tip: If you love audits, ISO is your jam.

COBIT (Control Objectives for Information and Related Technologies)

- Designed for aligning IT with business strategy
- Less "cyber geeky," more boardroom-friendly
- Helps tie security activities to actual business objectives

Think of COBIT as the translator between techies and suits.

Governance vs. Management — Wait, Aren't They the Same?

Not quite.

Governance	Management
Defines direction and policy	Executes plans and operations
Sets priorities and goals	Delivers on those goals
Concerned with accountability	Focused on performance
Owned by execs and board	Owned by IT/security leaders

You need both to succeed. One tells you where to go. The other gets you there.

Common Governance Fails (Let's Laugh... and Learn)

- **"We have policies. No one reads them."**

→ Write in plain language, summarize key points, and make them accessible.

- **"We do risk management... when the auditors show up."**

→ Make risk an ongoing convo, not a fire drill.

- **"The CISO reports to the IT manager."**

→ Nope. The CISO should have direct access to the board or execs. This isn't 2006.

- **"Security is a technical problem."**

→ It's a business problem with technical implications. Big difference.

Final Thoughts: Governance is the Grown-Up in the Room

Cybersecurity tools are cool. Threat intelligence is exciting. But without governance? It's like a team of action heroes with no mission, no plan, and no accountability.

"Governance keeps the chaos in check. It's not flashy. It's not fun. But it is what keeps your org from turning into a headline."

And if you ever hear someone say, "We don't need cybersecurity governance — we trust our people," feel free to laugh... and then hand them this chapter.

5.2 Developing and Enforcing Security Policies

"*Because shouting 'Don't click suspicious links!' over cubicle walls isn't an official security policy — it's just wishful thinking.*"

Let's face it: most employees think of security policies the same way they think of airplane safety instructions — "Nice to know, but I'll just wing it."

But here's the kicker: security policies are the foundation of your cybersecurity program. Without them, it's a free-for-all of rogue devices, reused passwords, and "confidential" docs being shared on Google Drive.

What Are Security Policies, Really?

In simple terms:

Security policies are documented rules and expectations that guide how people, processes, and tech should behave to protect the organization's assets.

They answer questions like:

- What's acceptable and what's not?
- Who can access what?
- How do we handle data?
- What happens when someone breaks the rules?

Think of them as the user manual for cybersecurity behavior — only slightly less fun than building IKEA furniture.

Key Characteristics of a Good Security Policy

Not all policies are created equal. A good one should be:

- **Clear & understandable** – No legalese or buzzword soup
- **Relevant to the organization** – Not just copied from a random template
- **Enforceable** – If you can't enforce it, don't write it
- **Aligned with business goals** – Not security for the sake of security
- **Supported by leadership** – Or it'll gather dust faster than a broken printer

Developing a Security Policy (Step-by-Step)

Let's break it down so you don't end up writing something only your cat reads.

1. Identify the Need

Start by understanding what the policy is solving:

- New regulation (like GDPR, HIPAA)
- A growing remote workforce
- Too many "oops" moments from employees
- Recent security incident (translation: "Let's not let that happen again...")

Pro tip: Don't create policies just because "we should have one." Tie it to a real business or risk need.

2. Engage Stakeholders

This ain't a solo mission. You need input from:

- IT & Security Teams
- Legal/Compliance
- HR (for employee stuff)
- Department heads (to avoid rules that break workflows)

Listen before you dictate. Otherwise, your policy might live in SharePoint and die in practice.

3. Draft the Policy

Keep it simple, direct, and no longer than it needs to be. Here's a basic structure:

- **Purpose** – Why this policy exists
- **Scope** – Who and what it applies to
- **Policy Statements** – The actual rules (e.g., "All employees must use MFA")
- **Roles & Responsibilities** – Who does what
- **Enforcement** – What happens if the rules are broken
- **Review Cycle** – When it'll be updated (annually is a good start)

Use plain language. If someone needs a law degree to understand it, rewrite it.

4. Review and Approve

Policies shouldn't surprise anyone. Share drafts, get feedback, revise, and then get formal approval from leadership or governance boards.

No exec buy-in = no enforcement = policy fail.

5. Communicate and Train

This is where a lot of policies go to die.

Don't just email the policy and call it a day. Instead:

- Announce it clearly and enthusiastically
- Include examples or FAQs
- Run short training sessions or include it in onboarding
- Use quizzes or gamification (because who doesn't love a good "Spot the Violation" game?)

Common Security Policies You Should Have

Here's a quick list of foundational policies most orgs need:

Acceptable Use Policy (AUP)

Defines proper use of company resources — what's OK and what's "uhhh, no."

Spoiler: torrenting movies on the company network = bad idea

Access Control Policy

Covers how access is granted, changed, and revoked. Includes least privilege, MFA, etc.

Remote Work Policy

Especially critical post-pandemic. Includes VPN usage, home Wi-Fi rules, and screen lock reminders.

Data Classification & Handling Policy

Tells people how to treat different data types: public, internal, confidential, restricted.

Because not all data deserves Fort Knox-level protection

Incident Response Policy

Outlines what happens when something goes wrong. Who reports? Who responds? Who freaks out?

Patch Management Policy

Ensures your systems get timely updates — and that one server isn't still running Windows XP

Enforcement: Making Sure It Actually Works

Policies are useless if no one follows them. So let's talk about enforcement.

Monitor & Audit

Use logs, alerts, and reports to check for violations. Not to be creepy — just to ensure people aren't "accidentally" emailing spreadsheets to their personal Gmail.

Tools Help

DLP systems, IAM platforms, and MDM solutions can help automate enforcement and reduce reliance on the honor system (which... let's be honest... isn't always reliable).

Consequences Matter

If there's no consequence for breaking the rules, the rules become suggestions. Be consistent and fair — and let HR handle the awkward conversations.

Reviewing and Updating Policies

Things change: new threats, new tools, new regulations, new... interns.

Set a regular review schedule — at least annually. But also update:

- After a security incident
- When new systems or tech roll out
- When regulations change (hello, GDPR v2.0)

Bonus: Have version control. Trust me, you don't want multiple people referencing "that one PDF from 2019."

Common Pitfalls (And How to Avoid Them)

Writing War and Peace

Keep it short and focused. No one wants to read a 40-page policy on screen savers.

Copy-pasting templates

Use them as a starting point, but customize for your business. A law firm and a pizza shop don't need the same security policies. (Unless it's a law firm that also sells pizza.)

No buy-in from staff

Explain why each policy matters. Make it relatable. Use examples from your own org — the weirder the better.

Outdated policies collecting digital dust

Review, update, and keep them alive. Dead policies won't protect you from live threats.

Final Thoughts: Policies Are the Rules of the Game

Think of your security policies like the rules of Monopoly:

- If everyone understands them, the game runs smoothly
- If people ignore them, someone flips the board and storms out

"You can have the best tech in the world — but without strong, enforced policies, you're building a cyber fortress with no doors, no locks, and a giant 'Welcome Hackers' sign."

So document wisely, train consistently, and enforce fairly.

5.3 Regulatory Compliance: GDPR, HIPAA, CCPA, PCI-DSS

"Welcome to the world of compliance, where the rules are made up, the fines are real, and yes, someone is always watching."

Regulatory compliance in cybersecurity is a lot like going to the dentist: not always fun, often expensive, and completely necessary if you want to avoid major pain down the road.

Whether you're dealing with customer data, health records, payment info, or just trying not to get dragged into court, regulatory compliance is your best friend. Or at least that one friend who keeps you out of trouble — but constantly reminds you to floss.

What is Regulatory Compliance?

In short, regulatory compliance means ensuring your organization follows all relevant laws, regulations, and standards that apply to data protection, privacy, and information security.

It's not just about being "secure" — it's about being legally secure. If cybersecurity is your shield, compliance is your armor — and if you skip it, lawsuits and fines come flying like arrows.

Why Compliance Matters

Let's break it down:

- **Legal Risk:** Violating laws like GDPR or HIPAA can lead to serious penalties — we're talking millions in fines.
- **Reputation Risk:** Customers lose trust fast if you mishandle their data.
- **Financial Risk:** Beyond fines, breaches can lead to lawsuits, lost revenue, and regulatory scrutiny.
- **Operational Risk:** Non-compliance often = weak controls = higher chance of getting breached.
- **And here's the kicker:** compliance ≠ security, but being non-compliant usually means you're also insecure.

Major Regulatory Frameworks (a.k.a. the Big Four)

Let's walk through the usual suspects you'll encounter depending on your business, location, and industry.

1. GDPR – General Data Protection Regulation (EU) ⍰⍰

"You better have a privacy notice, or the EU will notice."

What it is:

GDPR is a sweeping privacy law that applies to any organization handling the personal data of EU residents — even if your company is based on the other side of the planet.

Key Requirements:

- Get clear consent for data collection
- Allow data access, correction, and deletion ("right to be forgotten")
- Notify within 72 hours of a breach
- Appoint a Data Protection Officer (DPO) in some cases
- Keep data only as long as necessary

Penalties:

Up to €20 million or 4% of global annual turnover — whichever hurts more.

Pro tip:

Even if you're not in Europe, if you have EU visitors or customers... you're in scope.

2. HIPAA – Health Insurance Portability and Accountability Act (US)

"It's not just about keeping your medical data safe — it's about not letting Karen from HR accidentally email your blood test to the wrong department."

What it is:

HIPAA regulates how healthcare providers, insurers, and their business associates handle protected health information (PHI) in the U.S.

Key Rules:

- **Privacy Rule:** Sets the standards for protecting medical records and personal health info
- **Security Rule:** Defines technical and physical safeguards for electronic PHI (ePHI)
- **Breach Notification Rule:** You guessed it — notify affected individuals and HHS if there's a breach

Penalties:

Fines range from a slap on the wrist to $1.5 million+ per violation per year.

Pro tip:

If you handle any kind of health data — even indirectly — double-check your exposure to HIPAA. No one wants a HIPAA audit as a surprise party.

3. CCPA – California Consumer Privacy Act (US) ⯑

"Because what happens in California doesn't stay in California — it affects your whole website."

What it is:

CCPA gives California residents rights over their personal data, and it applies to many businesses that serve Californians, not just those based there.

Who it applies to:

- Businesses with $25M+ revenue
- Or those handling data on 100K+ consumers/households
- Or making over 50% of revenue from selling data

Key Rights:

- Know what data you're collecting
- Opt out of data selling
- Request deletion of their data
- Equal service regardless of privacy choices

Penalties:

- Up to $7,500 per intentional violation
- Plus class-action lawsuits from consumers

Pro tip:

Don't wait for the subpoena — get that cookie banner and privacy policy in order, ASAP.

4. PCI-DSS – Payment Card Industry Data Security Standard

"Swipe wrong, and you'll pay more than just the transaction fee."

What it is:

PCI-DSS is a security standard for any organization that stores, processes, or transmits credit card data.

Core Requirements (there are 12 in total):

- Use and maintain firewalls
- Encrypt cardholder data
- Use strong access controls
- Monitor and test networks regularly
- Restrict access based on business need

Levels of compliance:

Depends on transaction volume — but everyone needs to comply, even small e-commerce sites.

Penalties:

Fines from banks, loss of merchant privileges, and brand damage if you're breached.

Pro tip:

Outsource payment processing to PCI-compliant providers when possible — it's the ultimate "let someone else worry about it" move.

Mapping Compliance to Your Business

The trickiest part? Many companies fall under more than one regulation. You might be:

- **A U.S. company** → CCPA
- **Handling healthcare data** → HIPAA
- **Selling to Europeans** → GDPR
- **Accepting credit cards** → PCI-DSS

Yep — you might be in a compliance casserole.

That's why smart orgs:

- Conduct compliance audits
- Map regulatory controls to internal policies
- Use governance frameworks (like NIST, ISO 27001) to streamline across laws

Common Compliance Pitfalls (and How to Avoid Them)

Thinking compliance = checkbox exercise

Make it an ongoing part of operations — not a yearly panic project

Assuming you're "too small" to be targeted

Regulators and attackers don't care about your headcount

Ignoring third-party risk

You're responsible for what your vendors do with your data

Forgetting about training

If your team doesn't know the rules, how can they follow them?

Compliance Is a Journey, Not a Destination

Regulations evolve. New laws emerge. What worked last year may be outdated today. (Just like your "privacy policy" from 2016 that hasn't seen daylight since Obama was in office.)

"The best compliance strategy? Stay informed, stay adaptable, and build your security with laws in mind — not just as an afterthought."

You don't have to love compliance, but if you respect it, it'll keep your business safe, legal, and out of the headlines.

5.4 Auditing and Reporting Procedures

*"**Welcome to the thrilling world of audits** — where everything you've ever done is questioned, your documentation is judged, and someone finally notices that outdated password policy from 2014."*

If regulatory compliance is the rulebook, auditing and reporting are the referee's whistle — calling fouls, checking playbooks, and occasionally throwing flags on sketchy activity.

But fear not. Audits aren't here to make your life miserable (even if it feels like it during Q4). They're here to keep your cybersecurity program honest, measurable, and continuously improving. And no, hiding under your desk won't make them go away.

So... What Exactly Is an Audit?

In cyber terms, an audit is a structured process to evaluate whether your security controls, processes, and documentation are aligned with internal policies and external regulations.

There are two types:

- **Internal audits** – Done by your own team (or friendly consultants)
- **External audits** – Done by third parties, often for certifications or regulatory compliance (a.k.a. "the real deal")

Think of audits like your annual health check-up:

- A bit awkward
- Slightly uncomfortable
- Incredibly necessary to catch small problems before they become system-wide meltdowns

Reporting, on the Other Hand...

While audits focus on what is, reporting tells the story of what's happening — and helps you make better decisions. It involves:

- Logging incidents
- Documenting responses
- Measuring KPIs (Key Performance Indicators)
- Reporting breaches (when necessary)
- Tracking compliance over time

Done right, reporting = clarity. Done wrong, it = 700 pages of "data" that nobody reads.

The Auditing Process (Simplified for Human Beings)

Let's walk through what a typical cybersecurity audit looks like — without falling asleep halfway through.

1. Planning and Scoping

Before any digging starts, the audit team defines:

- **What's being audited** (systems, processes, departments)
- **Timeframe** (last quarter? full year?)
- **Relevant frameworks** (NIST, ISO 27001, PCI-DSS, etc.)
- **Who needs to be involved** (Pro tip: everyone eventually)

Tip: Prepare a list of assets, stakeholders, previous audit reports, and documentation in advance. It'll save your bacon later.

2. Data Collection

This is where the fun begins. Auditors will want:

- Policies and procedures
- Logs and access records
- Incident response plans
- Evidence of security training
- Vulnerability scans and patch history
- System configs and user permissions

Translation: They'll ask for everything you've ever promised to do security-wise — and receipts, please.

3. Interviews and Observations

Expect questions like:

- "Who has admin access?"
- "How often do you review logs?"
- "Where is your disaster recovery plan?"
- "What's your favorite brand of coffee?" (Okay, not that one... probably)

They may also observe live processes or test your backup restore procedures.

It's like being on a reality show, but with more firewalls and fewer dance-offs.

4. Gap Analysis

Here's where auditors compare your current setup against:

- Your internal policies
- Industry standards
- Applicable regulations

They'll identify:

- **Strengths** (hooray!)
- **Gaps** (boo!)
- **Risks** (double boo!)
- **Recommendations** (aka homework)

5. Reporting the Results

Once the audit is complete, you'll get an audit report, which includes:

- Executive summary
- Methodology
- Findings (good and bad)
- Risk rankings (low, medium, high)
- Remediation recommendations

Timelines for fixes

If external, this might be submitted to regulators, clients, or even published in an annual report (hello, transparency).

Metrics to Report (Without Making Everyone Cry)

You don't need to measure everything — just the stuff that matters. Here are key cybersecurity metrics that should show up in your reporting dashboards:

- Number of vulnerabilities detected vs. remediated
- Mean time to detect/respond (MTTD/MTTR)
- Access control violations
- Policy compliance rates

- Number of incidents reported (and resolved)
- Security training participation and test results
- Breach attempts vs. successful intrusions

Keep it visual. Use charts, graphs, and color-coding — because no one wants to decode 12 pages of raw CSV tables before their first coffee.

Keeping Audit Trails (Because "I Swear I Did That" Won't Cut It)

Audit trails are detailed records of system and user activities. They're vital for:

- Proving compliance
- Investigating incidents
- Preventing fraud
- Reconstructing what happened post-incident

Pro tip: Use centralized logging systems (like SIEM platforms) to collect, store, and analyze audit logs. Bonus points for alerts and automated reports. ◈

Breach Reporting: The Clock is Ticking

If you suffer a data breach, reporting it correctly and on time is mission-critical.

Here's how it generally works:

- **GDPR:** Notify within 72 hours
- **HIPAA:** Notify affected individuals within 60 days
- **CCPA:** Must notify if breach affects 500+ California residents
- **PCI-DSS:** Notify your payment processor immediately

Don't try to hide it. That never ends well — regulators will find out eventually, and fines will double if they do.

Common Mistakes in Auditing & Reporting

Let's cover what not to do, shall we?

Being unprepared

Solution: Keep documentation up to date — don't wait until auditors knock

Overpromising, underperforming

Don't write "we patch all systems weekly" in your policy if you haven't patched the marketing server since 2021

Manual reporting

Use dashboards, automation tools, and scheduled reports. Google Sheets won't save you when things get chaotic.

Lack of accountability

Assign owners for each control. If "everyone's responsible," then no one is.

How to Make Life Easier Next Audit Season

Create an audit calendar

Mark recurring tasks, reviews, and key compliance deadlines

Use frameworks as your foundation

NIST CSF, ISO 27001, COBIT — these help structure both controls and audits

Keep records centralized

Use a GRC tool or internal wiki to organize documents, policies, logs, and evidence

Practice mini-audits

Don't wait for the big show. Run quarterly checks or "audit drills" so you're always ready

Train your teams

Make sure IT, DevOps, HR, and execs know what auditors might ask — and how to answer without panic in their eyes

Final Thoughts: Audits Aren't Enemies, They're Tune-Ups

Audits may not be glamorous, but they are incredibly powerful tools for understanding how secure (or insecure) your organization truly is.

"An audit is not about catching people messing up — it's about making sure your defenses are as strong as you think they are."

So don't dread it — own it. Use audits and reporting as part of your continuous improvement plan. Get organized, stay transparent, and keep your logs clean.

And if all else fails... bribe the auditor with coffee and cookies. (Just kidding... unless it works.)

5.5 Ethics in Cybersecurity and Risk Management

"*To hack or not to hack... that is the ethical question.*"

*(**Also:** Should I report that bug... or sell it on the dark web and buy a boat?)*

Cybersecurity isn't just about technology — it's about people. And when people are involved, things can get messy. Welcome to the wild and often overlooked world of ethics in cybersecurity and risk management, where you're constantly walking the line between what's legal, what's moral, and what's just plain shady.

Sure, firewalls and frameworks are cool, but what happens when you're faced with a situation where doing the right thing conflicts with your boss's orders? Or when cutting corners means getting ahead faster?

Spoiler alert: Ethics isn't always black and white — but your decisions still paint a very real picture.

What Do We Mean by "Ethics" Anyway?

In cybersecurity, ethics refers to the moral principles and standards of behavior that govern how we protect, manage, and interact with data, systems, and people.

It's about doing the right thing, even when:

- Nobody is watching ()
- There's no regulation forcing you to
- Or when the unethical choice might be easier or more profitable

Think of ethics as the internal compass of cybersecurity. Without it, you're just a hacker in a hoodie waiting to be featured in a Netflix docuseries.

Common Ethical Dilemmas in Cybersecurity

Let's look at some real-world gray areas that make professionals scratch their heads (and sometimes consult a lawyer).

1. Responsible Disclosure vs. Selling Vulnerabilities

You find a major zero-day vulnerability in a widely used product. Now what?

- Do you tell the vendor privately and give them time to patch it? (Responsible)
- Do you go public to force change? (Risky)
- Or do you sell it on a dark web forum for six figures? (Unethical, illegal, but unfortunately... common)

The ethical move: disclose responsibly through coordinated channels like CERTs or bug bounty programs.

Bonus points: You might still get paid. Just... without the FBI knocking on your door at 3AM.

2. Monitoring Employees

Your job is to keep the network safe. But that means you could technically read emails, monitor chats, or see someone's browser history from two weeks ago...

Just because you can, does that mean you should?

Rule of thumb: Only collect and access what's necessary, and always inform employees about what's being monitored. Transparency = trust.

Also, nobody needs to see 3 hours of YouTube cat videos during work hours.

3. Penetration Testing and Social Engineering

When testing systems, you're often allowed to hack your own company. But what about tricking the receptionist with a fake delivery? Or impersonating the CEO?

Is it ethical to lie for security testing purposes?

Yes — if:

- It's agreed upon in the scope of work
- The organization consents
- It's documented and evaluated

No — if you're just winging it without approval. That's not ethical hacking — that's just being a sneaky jerk with admin rights.

4. Bias in Risk Scoring and AI Tools

More organizations use AI and automation to flag risks and scan user behavior. But what if:

- The system disproportionately flags certain groups?
- It blocks legitimate users based on flawed logic?
- Or it's trained on biased data?

Ethics says: Just because it's machine-generated doesn't mean it's morally neutral.

Always test for fairness, transparency, and accountability in your tools — because biased bots are still your responsibility.

The Pillars of Ethical Cybersecurity

Let's break it down to the moral DNA of every cybersecurity pro:

1. Confidentiality

You're entrusted with private info. Guard it like it's your grandma's secret cookie recipe.

2. Integrity

Be honest — about incidents, vulnerabilities, risks, and your own mistakes. If you mess up, own it. (Then patch it.)

3. Accountability

You're not a ghost. Your actions (or inactions) have real impact. Take responsibility and make decisions you can stand behind.

4. Transparency

Explain what you're doing and why. If your security feels like a magic trick, you're probably doing it wrong (or hiding something).

5. Respect for Privacy

Protect users not just from hackers, but from overreach. Yes, even from your marketing department.

Codes of Ethics You Should Actually Read (At Least Once)

Here are a few formal ethical frameworks that cybersecurity professionals follow:

- **(ISC)² Code of Ethics** – Used by CISSP and other cert holders
- **ISACA Code of Professional Ethics** – For CISA, CISM, etc.
- **SANS Cyber Ethics Resources** – Lots of good reading material
- **ACM/IEEE Codes** – Tech-heavy but relevant

They all boil down to: Be honest. Do no harm. Protect the public. Stay competent. And please, don't be evil (Google took that one already).

Ethics in Risk Management Decisions

When you're assessing risk, ethics isn't just a bonus — it's baked in:

- Don't bury findings because they're inconvenient
- Don't downplay likelihood or impact just to look good
- Don't favor profits over people's safety or privacy

Remember: Good risk management isn't just about reducing losses — it's about protecting what matters most. And that includes trust.

Ethical Risk = Real Risk

Unethical behavior has a nasty habit of becoming a headline:

- Facebook and Cambridge Analytica

- Uber's cover-up of a data breach
- Snowden's revelations about government surveillance

These aren't just scandals — they're cautionary tales of ignoring ethical red flags.

Don't be the next case study.

Embedding Ethics in Your Culture

Want to be the team that does the right thing even when it's hard? Here's how:

- Train employees on ethics, not just compliance
- Encourage whistleblowing (safely and anonymously)
- Review policies through an ethical lens — not just a legal one
- Foster a speak-up culture where people can question questionable stuff

Ethics isn't just a checklist. It's the soul of your security strategy.

Final Thoughts: The Right Thing is Usually the Harder Thing

Let's face it: the ethical choice is often slower, more expensive, and less convenient. But it's also the one that builds trust, protects users, and keeps you off Reddit's front page for all the wrong reasons.

"Cybersecurity without ethics is just control. With ethics, it becomes protection."

So next time you're faced with a decision that makes you squirm a little... pause. Reflect. Then do the right thing.

And if all else fails? Ask yourself:

"Would I be cool explaining this on the news?"

If the answer's no... maybe rethink it.

Chapter 6: Incident Response and Recovery

Picture this: it's 3 a.m., your phone is buzzing, your server's been breached, and someone's Twitter account now has a Bitcoin address in the bio. Welcome to Incident Response, where cyber nightmares come to life and coffee becomes a food group. Don't worry—we're building your panic plan before you panic.

In this chapter, we walk through the full lifecycle of cyber incident response and recovery. From developing a solid incident response plan to containment, investigation, and recovery strategies, you'll gain insight into how to manage crises effectively. Post-incident reviews and lessons learned are also covered to ensure continuous improvement.

6.1 Building an Incident Response Plan (IRP)

"They say failing to plan is planning to fail... and in cybersecurity, it's also how you end up in front of a boardroom sweating through your shirt while explaining why the entire customer database is on Pastebin."

Welcome to the world of Incident Response — where chaos meets calm, and your plan is the only thing standing between a minor hiccup and a full-blown cyber meltdown.

If you're thinking, "We'll deal with it when it happens," then congratulations — you've just volunteered for a starring role in the next cybersecurity horror story.

Let's fix that by creating a solid, human-friendly, and actually usable Incident Response Plan (IRP).

What Is an IRP and Why Should You Care?

An Incident Response Plan is your structured, step-by-step playbook for detecting, responding to, managing, and recovering from a cybersecurity incident.

Think of it as your fire drill for digital disasters. You don't wait for flames to start practicing how to leave the building, right? (Right?)

A good IRP can:

- Minimize damage
- Reduce recovery time and costs
- Preserve evidence
- Keep regulators and customers off your back
- Prevent sheer panic and wild finger-pointing

The 6 Core Phases of an IRP

Let's break it down into the essential steps — also known as the "SANS Incident Response Lifecycle," which is kind of like the Avengers of incident management.

1. Preparation

This phase is all about getting your ducks in a row before things go sideways.

Key elements:

- Form your incident response team (IT, security, legal, PR, HR)
- Define roles and responsibilities

- Write down who calls who when stuff hits the fan
- Draft templates for communication (emails, press releases, incident logs)
- Establish secure channels for internal response coordination (no, Slack DMs don't count)

Pro tip: Run tabletop exercises. It's like Dungeons & Dragons for security nerds — but instead of slaying orcs, you're fighting ransomware.

2. Identification

Time to spot the digital smoke before the servers burn.

In this phase, you:

- Detect anomalous activity (through logs, SIEMs, alerts, user reports)
- Confirm whether it's really an incident (vs. a broken printer, which — while annoying — is not cybercrime)
- Categorize and prioritize the event

Common types of incidents:

- Phishing attacks
- Malware infections
- Insider threats
- DDoS attacks
- Data breaches

SPEED MATTERS. THE sooner you detect, the sooner you can respond — and the fewer gray hairs you'll grow in the process.

3. Containment

Your goal here? Stop the bleeding.

Containment is about isolating the threat without shutting down the entire business like it's Y2K all over again.

Two types:

- **Short-term containment:** Disconnect infected systems, block IPs, disable accounts.
- **Long-term containment:** Apply patches, reset credentials, and prepare for recovery — without letting the attacker back in.

Reminder: Don't just pull the plug. You might need forensic evidence later.

4. Eradication

Now that the fire's out, it's time to clean up the mess.

What to do:

- Remove malware or unauthorized access
- Delete malicious accounts
- Fix exploited vulnerabilities
- Rebuild compromised systems (preferably from clean images)

It's like disinfecting a wound — skip this step, and you're just asking for reinfection.

5. Recovery

Dust off, reboot, and cautiously return to normal.

Steps include:

- Restoring systems from backups
- Monitoring systems for signs of re-compromise
- Gradually reintroducing affected systems to production

Trust, but verify. Just because it looks fine doesn't mean your attacker didn't leave behind a nasty surprise.

Aim: Get back to business while keeping security tighter than your jeans after the holidays.

6. Lessons Learned

Congratulations — you survived! Now let's make sure it doesn't happen again.

After-action reviews should include:

- What happened?
- How did we respond?
- What worked?
- What failed?
- How can we improve?

Update your IRP based on this incident, and share the insights with the team. Even the ugly parts.

Bonus: turn lessons learned into security awareness training so everyone else learns too (and not just from the memes in your incident Slack channel).

What Should Your IRP Contain?

Here's a quick checklist of IRP components you'll want in your plan:

- Contact lists (internal teams, vendors, legal, law enforcement)
- Defined incident categories and severity levels
- Roles and responsibilities matrix
- Communication plans (internal & external)
- Step-by-step procedures for each response phase
- Log retention and evidence handling policies
- Compliance and reporting obligations (like GDPR breach notification timers)
- Testing and update schedules

If your IRP is a 95-page PDF no one has read since 2019, it's not a plan — it's a paperweight.

Tools to Help You Respond Like a Pro

You don't need to go full Mission: Impossible. Just get the basics right:

- **SIEMs (e.g., Splunk, QRadar, Sentinel):** to monitor, detect, alert
- **EDR/XDR (e.g., CrowdStrike, SentinelOne):** to contain and eradicate
- **Case management systems:** to document everything
- **Communication tools:** secure chat, war room Zoom, encrypted email
- **Backup and recovery tools:** to bring things back from the dead

Bonus if your coffee machine is also on the response team.

Common Mistakes to Avoid

- **No defined roles** — "Who's in charge?" is not a question you want to ask mid-breach
- **Delayed detection** — hours matter, days kill
- **Poor communication** — silence creates chaos (and lawsuits)
- **Lack of testing** — untested plans = wishful thinking

- **Forgetting compliance** — regulators don't accept "oops" as a valid excuse

Final Thoughts: Plan Like It's Inevitable (Because It Kinda Is)

Cyber incidents are like thunderstorms — you can't stop them, but you can carry an umbrella.

Your Incident Response Plan is that umbrella: ready, reliable, and maybe a little bit over-engineered (which is exactly how we like it in security).

"When the breach hits, the worst time to write a plan is during the breach."

So build your IRP now, test it often, keep it updated, and maybe — just maybe — the next time chaos comes knocking, you'll meet it with a calm smile and a clipboard.

6.2 Detection and Containment Strategies

"If a cyber attack hits your network and nobody's monitoring the logs... did it really happen? (Spoiler: Yes. And now your data's for sale.)"

In cybersecurity, you can't defend what you can't detect, and you definitely can't contain what you don't know is spreading. That's why detection and containment are the dynamic duo of incident response — kind of like Batman and Robin, but with firewalls and packet sniffers instead of capes and grappling hooks.

This chapter is all about sharpening your Spidey-senses for threats and locking things down like Fort Knox the moment something sketchy slips in. Because in a world where breaches are inevitable, speed is your superpower.

Part 1: Detection – Catch It Before It Wrecks It

What Is Detection in Cybersecurity?

Detection is your system's ability to recognize when something fishy — or downright dangerous — is happening. It's the early-warning siren that screams, "Hey, someone's trying to log in from Uzbekistan at 3AM... again."

Goal: Spot malicious activity as early as possible so you can respond before attackers finish their evil PowerPoint presentation on how they pwned your network.

Tools of the Detection Trade

Here's your arsenal of sensors and detectors — use them wisely, and use them often:

- **SIEM (Security Information and Event Management):** Aggregates logs from across your systems and raises alerts when something's weird (like your printer suddenly scanning your payroll database).

- **EDR (Endpoint Detection and Response):** Watches endpoints like a hawk for malware, behavioral anomalies, and shady processes.

- **NDR (Network Detection and Response):** Sniffs out suspicious traffic across your network — because attackers love hiding in the noise.

- **Intrusion Detection Systems (IDS):** These detect known attack patterns and anomalies. Signature-based, behavior-based, or hybrid — all have their place.

- **Honey Pots/Deception Tools:** Fake assets meant to lure in attackers like moths to a flame (except this flame logs everything and sends it straight to your SOC).

Detection Techniques

Let's talk strategy. How do you spot the bad guys in the first place?

- **Log Analysis** – Check logs for anomalies: failed login attempts, privilege escalations, rogue scripts, weird DNS lookups.

- **User and Entity Behavior Analytics (UEBA)** – AI/ML-powered tools that say, "Hey, Bob in accounting doesn't usually download 10GB of files at 2AM."

- **Threat Hunting** – Proactive. Manual. Ninja-level. Analysts actively look for signs of compromise before alerts fire.

Threat Intelligence Integration – Feeds from external sources (like abuse.ch or MISP) help you detect emerging threats by IP, hash, or domain.

Common Indicators of Compromise (IOCs)

Keep your eyes peeled for:

- Unusual outbound traffic

- Unauthorized file access

- Suspicious login times or locations

- Unexpected system restarts or configuration changes

- Sudden CPU spikes or new processes

- Files named something like "donotdelete_final_version2_reallyfinal.exe"

If it feels off, investigate it. Worst case? False positive. Best case? You just stopped a ransomware attack.

Part 2: Containment – Lock It Down, Fast

So you detected the threat — now what? You contain it like it's a rabid raccoon in your data center.

The goal of containment is simple:

Stop the attack from spreading while preserving evidence and minimizing damage.

Types of Containment

Short-Term Containment

Act fast to limit the blast radius.

- Isolate infected systems from the network

- Disable compromised user accounts

- Block malicious IPs/domains

- Revoke or rotate credentials

Speed matters. Every second the attacker remains connected = more risk. Think of it like yanking the Ethernet cord, but with precision and slightly less panic.

Long-Term Containment

Once things are under control, move to long-term fixes that prepare you for recovery.

- Patch exploited vulnerabilities
- Reimage compromised systems
- Apply compensating controls (e.g., stricter firewall rules)
- Implement temporary monitoring on high-risk assets

This is where you play chess, not checkers. Strategic moves now can save you future facepalms.

Containment Do's and Don'ts

Do:

- Document every action you take
- Inform key stakeholders
- Involve legal/compliance if data loss is suspected
- Preserve logs and disk images if forensic analysis may be needed

Don't:

- Panic and shut down all systems
- Wipe machines before analyzing them (unless ransomware, then maybe... but ask an expert first)
- Forget to communicate — internal silence can be just as damaging as the breach itself

Air Gapping – Cybersecurity's Panic Button

In extreme cases (think nation-state APT or full-blown ransomware), you might go nuclear and air gap — physically or logically disconnect affected systems from the network.

This should be your "break glass in case of emergency" move — it works, but it's disruptive and might trigger attacker countermeasures. Use it wisely.

Real-Life Example: Fast Containment Saves the Day

Scenario: A company notices strange outbound traffic going to an IP in Russia. The SIEM raises an alert. SOC investigates and finds a remote access trojan (RAT) active on an HR manager's machine.

What worked:

- Detection via network anomaly rules
- Immediate short-term containment (endpoint isolated)

- Incident declared; IR team steps in
- Malware analyzed, and source determined to be a phishing attachment
- Long-term containment via patching and policy updates

Result: No data exfiltration. No breach notification. Just a well-handled incident and a slightly embarrassed HR manager now banned from opening cat meme attachments.

Final Thoughts: Early Birds & Fast Hands Win

Detection and containment aren't just technical steps — they're your frontline defense. Miss them, and every other phase of incident response becomes a desperate cleanup job.

"The faster you detect, the smaller the mess. The faster you contain, the shorter the apology tour."

Stay alert. Stay ready. And make sure your IR team isn't just on-call — they're caffeinated, trained, and equipped for action.

6.3 Digital Forensics and Investigation

"Digital forensics: because asking the hacker politely what they did usually doesn't work."

Welcome to the CSI of cyberspace — Digital Forensics and Investigation, where we don't use fingerprint dust, but we do use Wireshark, memory dumps, and a level of log obsession that borders on romance.

This chapter isn't just about finding out what happened — it's about figuring out how, when, where, who (if we're lucky), and how bad. And yes, unlike TV, it takes more than 60 minutes and a dramatic zoom into the monitor.

What Is Digital Forensics?

In simple terms, digital forensics is the science of collecting, preserving, analyzing, and presenting digital evidence. In an incident response context, it's how we:

- Investigate security breaches
- Identify attack vectors
- Trace attacker activity
- Determine the scope and impact
- Support potential legal actions or compliance requirements

Basically, if your systems have been compromised, forensics is how you reverse-engineer the crime scene and prove what went down.

Think Sherlock Holmes — but instead of footprints and cigar ash, you're dealing with timestamps, log entries, and TCP headers.

The Digital Forensics Process

Just like a real investigation, digital forensics follows a systematic approach:

1. Identification

Before you can analyze anything, you need to know what to look at.

This involves:

- Identifying compromised systems or suspicious behavior
- Listing all potentially impacted assets (servers, endpoints, mobile devices, cloud environments)
- Prioritizing which systems are most critical for evidence collection

You don't want to start wiping systems or patching before pulling forensics — otherwise, say goodbye to crucial evidence.

2. Preservation

Evidence can be fragile in the digital world — logs rotate, memory clears, and attackers love to cover their tracks.

The key is to preserve the scene:

- **Make forensic disk images** (bit-by-bit clones of drives)
- **Dump RAM** (for volatile data like processes, keys, network connections)
- **Collect relevant logs** (system, security, firewall, SIEM, etc.)
- **Isolate affected systems** (but don't power them off unless necessary!)

Rule #1: Touch nothing unless you're capturing it. You're not fixing yet — you're freezing.

3. Collection

This is the part where you become an elite digital vacuum cleaner.

You'll want to gather:

- File system metadata (timestamps, ownership)
- Running processes and services
- Registry keys (on Windows)
- Network connections and DNS queries
- Installed software
- Event logs and audit trails
- Email headers and attachments

Use proper tools like:

- FTK Imager
- EnCase
- Volatility (for memory analysis)
- Autopsy
- Wireshark
- Sleuth Kit

- Sysinternals Suite

And always — always — follow the chain of custody protocols. That means logging who touches the evidence and when. If this ends up in court, sloppy handling = lost case.

4. Analysis

Alright, now the fun part: connecting the dots.

This is where you sift through the data, logs, and artifacts to figure out:

- **What happened?** (e.g., malware infection, privilege escalation)
- **How did it happen?** (e.g., phishing email, open RDP port, zero-day exploit)
- **What did they access/do?** (e.g., downloaded data, created users, installed backdoors)
- **When did it occur?** (timeline reconstruction is key!)
- **Is the threat still active?** (because round two could be in progress...)

A few analysis techniques:

- Timeline analysis (e.g., using Plaso or Timesketch)
- File hashing to detect tampering
- Signature-based malware detection
- Behavior analysis (e.g., unusual scripts, lateral movement)
- Data exfiltration monitoring (upload spikes, cloud transfers, etc.)

5. Reporting

Ah, yes — the part where your keyboard detective work turns into something your boss, legal team, and maybe law enforcement can read.

A good digital forensics report includes:

- Executive summary (for non-tech folks)
- Timeline of events
- Detailed technical findings
- Impact assessment (what was compromised)
- Attacker attribution (if possible — often hard)
- Screenshots, logs, hash values

- Recommendations for remediation

Pro tip: Avoid jargon soup. Nobody wants to read "correlated anomalous mutex values in PID 1192." Translate your tech wizardry into clear insight.

Common Artifacts to Look For

When investigating an incident, these are your digital breadcrumbs:

Artifact Type	Example Clues
File system changes	New files, modified timestamps, suspicious .exes
Memory dumps	Running malware, encryption keys, C2 connections
Network logs	Data exfiltration, suspicious IPs, odd ports
Registry keys	Persistence mechanisms, autostart entries
Web browser history	Phishing sites visited, downloads
Log files	Failed login attempts, system reboots

It's not just what's there — it's what's been changed, hidden, or deleted.

Legal and Ethical Considerations

Let's not forget: digital forensics can involve sensitive data — employee emails, internal documents, even personal files.

Best practices:

- Respect privacy laws (GDPR, HIPAA, etc.)
- Get appropriate authorizations before accessing personal devices
- Secure your evidence storage (encrypted, access-controlled)
- Always maintain the chain of custody

Remember: you're not just a hacker hunter — you're also a digital lawyer-in-training.

Common Mistakes in Digital Investigations

Don't be that team. Avoid these:

- Powering off the system without capturing RAM
- Tampering with files before cloning disks
- Failing to timestamp logs in UTC
- Forgetting to document your actions

- Using production systems for analysis (yikes)

Digital evidence doesn't get a second chance — one wrong move and it's toast.

Case Snapshot: Rootkit Rumble

A financial firm noticed that some employees were locked out of their accounts — and $5M mysteriously disappeared in crypto transfers.

Investigation revealed:

- An advanced rootkit planted via a phishing PDF
- The attacker created fake admin accounts
- Keystrokes were logged for weeks
- Transfers were automated during weekends

Forensics team used memory dumps, registry inspection, and timeline reconstruction to piece it all together.

Outcome: Rootkit removed, accounts recovered, law enforcement looped in with a solid evidence package.

Also: the IT guy finally got approval to block macros in email attachments. Victory.

Final Thoughts: Be Curious. Be Careful. Be Complete.

Digital forensics isn't just about finding "the bad guy." It's about telling the whole truth — what happened, how it happened, and what we can learn from it.

"In a cybercrime, every byte is a witness, and every log entry has a story."

So keep your tools sharp, your instincts sharper, and remember — forensics isn't just about solving the mystery, it's about making sure it never happens again.

6.4 Recovery and Business Continuity Planning

"Recovery planning is like flossing — nobody enjoys it, but skip it long enough and things fall apart."

So, the digital apocalypse hit. Malware danced through your systems, data ran for the hills, alarms were blaring, and your team pulled three all-nighters fueled by cold coffee and sheer panic. Now what?

Recovery and Business Continuity Planning (BCP) is where the dust settles and the real work begins: getting back online without losing your sanity (or your job). In this chapter, we focus on how to bounce back — stronger, faster, and ideally with fewer tears next time.

What's Recovery, Anyway?

Recovery is getting your systems and services back to operational status after a cyber incident. It's not just flipping the switch back on — it's about doing so safely, cleanly, and without letting the attacker back in for round two.

BCP, on the other hand, is the wider umbrella: it's your plan for keeping the business running even when things go sideways. It includes IT recovery, yes — but also covers communication, operations, and those good ol' things like payroll and supply chains.

Core Components of Recovery Planning

Here's what your post-incident recovery toolkit needs:

1. Eradication Complete

Before recovery even starts, you better be 100% sure the threat is gone:

- Malware fully removed?
- Backdoors closed?
- Compromised accounts disabled or reset?
- Logs reviewed to confirm no lateral movement?
- Recovering before eradicating is like cleaning up a flooded room without fixing the leak.

2. Recovery Objectives: RTO & RPO

Let's talk acronyms that'll make or break your recovery:

RTO (Recovery Time Objective):

How quickly do you need systems back online before it becomes a disaster?

Example: We must restore email access within 2 hours.

RPO (Recovery Point Objective):

How much data can you afford to lose (measured in time)?

Example: We can tolerate losing only 30 minutes of transactions.

These objectives shape your backup frequency, failover designs, and cloud strategy. Set them realistically — not "ASAP" or "before Steve in Sales notices."

3. Data Recovery: Bring Back the Bits

This is where you break out the backups and hope to all that is good in cybersecurity that:

- They're recent
- They weren't infected
- You actually tested them at least once this year

You'll likely restore from:

- Full system images
- Incremental backups
- Cloud snapshots
- Offline (air-gapped) storage

Pro tip: Isolate recovered systems and monitor them closely. Don't let a backup become your second infection.

4. System Restoration: Not Just a Reboot

You can't just reinstall Windows and call it a day. You need to:

- Harden systems (disable unused services, apply secure configs)
- Re-patch everything (including what was exploited)
- Re-deploy security controls (EDR, antivirus, firewalls)
- Recreate user accounts with fresh creds
- Validate integrations (make sure apps still talk to each other)
- Run test traffic and simulated transactions to verify

Then — and only then — open the gates.

5. User Communication & Stakeholder Updates

Imagine logging in after a breach and seeing only a blue screen. You'd panic, right?

Communication is key:

- Let employees know what's happening (and when systems will be back)
- Update customers (honesty > silence)
- Alert legal, compliance, PR, execs

Bonus: Keep a few canned message templates ready for these scenarios — nobody writes great copy mid-crisis.

Business Continuity Planning (BCP)

Now zoom out. What if the recovery takes a week? Or your HQ loses internet? Or cloud services go down during peak hours?

BCP ensures you don't go belly-up during disruptions. It's your game plan for resilience.

BCP Covers:

- Critical Business Functions (e.g., order processing, payroll, client onboarding)
- Alternative Workflows (manual processes, remote access, phone orders)
- Personnel Roles & Responsibilities during a crisis
- Alternate Communication Channels (when email's dead, use Slack, phones, or semaphore flags)
- Third-Party Dependencies (vendors, cloud providers, supply chains)
- Backup Facilities or Remote Work Options

You're not just recovering IT — you're keeping the business breathing.

Writing a BCP Plan (Without Boring People to Death)

Here's what a solid BCP includes:

1. Executive Summary (short and readable, promise)
2. Scope & Objectives
3. Business Impact Analysis Summary
4. Critical Processes and Systems
5. Recovery Strategies
6. Team Roles and Contacts
7. Communication Plan
8. Testing & Maintenance Procedures

Bonus: Stick a humorously named coffee stash and emergency pizza vendor list in there for morale.

Test It or Forget It

If your plan lives in a dusty folder named "Contingency_FINAL_final_v3.docx," it's useless.

You must test your recovery and BCP:

- Run tabletop exercises ("What if email is down for 48 hours?")
- Do partial failovers or simulated outages
- Restore from backups regularly
- Involve departments beyond IT (finance, HR, marketing — they all panic too)

Don't wait for a crisis to find out your backup from 2021 was just a corrupted zip file.

Real-World Example: A Company That Recovered Right

Case Study: A retail chain got hit with ransomware the night before Black Friday (yeah, nightmare fuel).

They:

- Detected it early thanks to EDR alerts
- Had daily backups in cold storage
- Switched to alternate payment systems at stores
- Used SMS to notify staff (email was down)
- Recovered systems within 24 hours
- Issued a transparent press statement and gained customer trust

Because they tested their recovery plan, they didn't just survive — they came out looking like pros.

Final Thoughts: Don't Just Hope It Works

Hope is not a strategy. Recovery and BCP are your business seatbelts — you never want to need them, but when you do, they better work without squeaking.

"In cybersecurity, it's not 'if' you'll fall — it's whether you land on a safety net or faceplant into chaos."

So make the plan. Test the plan. Update the plan. And give your team a big high five when it saves the day.

6.5 Post-Incident Review and Improvement

"Congrats, you survived the cyberattack! Now it's time to sit down, relive the trauma, and politely ask everyone what went wrong."

If recovery was about getting back on your feet, post-incident review is where you ask, "How did I trip in the first place?" and "How can I avoid faceplanting again?" This final (but absolutely crucial) phase of the incident response cycle isn't just a debrief — it's your chance to turn a nightmare into knowledge.

Let's be real: no matter how airtight you thought your defenses were, if you experienced an incident, something slipped. Could be a misconfigured firewall, an overlooked alert, or the classic "Dave clicked another email with the subject line 'Free Pizza.'"

Let's dig in.

What is a Post-Incident Review?

Also known as a Lessons Learned meeting or After Action Report (AAR), this is a structured evaluation of the entire incident lifecycle. You'll:

- Review what happened and why
- Assess how well the response went
- Identify gaps in detection, communication, or mitigation
- Document takeaways and action items
- Improve processes, policies, and training

Think of it as your cybersecurity therapy session. Except there's a lot more paperwork and fewer scented candles.

Why Bother With This Step?

Skipping this phase is like finishing a fire drill and saying, "Well, we didn't burn down. Let's never talk about it again."

Here's what you gain from a solid post-incident review:

- Improved future response times
- Fixing root causes
- Better cross-team coordination
- Compliance brownie points (auditors love documented reviews)
- Increased stakeholder confidence
- Learning from your pain, so you don't repeat it

And let's be honest, nothing beats the satisfaction of creating a spreadsheet that proves exactly how and why Steve's "password123" was not, in fact, a good idea.

Anatomy of a Great Post-Incident Review

Let's break it down into digestible parts:

1. Create an Incident Timeline

Build a chronological map from start to finish. Use:

- Logs (SIEM, firewall, system)
- Alerting tools (EDR, IDS)
- Emails and tickets
- Manual notes from responders

Map out:

- When the breach started
- When it was detected
- How it was escalated
- What actions were taken (and when)
- When recovery began and completed

Goal: Identify dwell time, response time, and any delays or miscommunications.

2. Who Did What, and When?

Get input from:

- Security teams
- IT support
- Comms/PR
- Legal
- Business unit leaders

Ask each group:

- What did you know?
- When did you know it?

- What actions did you take?
- What worked and what didn't?

It's not about blame — it's about clarity. (Okay, mostly not about blame.)

3. Root Cause Analysis

Ask the Five Whys (yes, like an annoying toddler):

- Why was the system compromised?
- Why was that vulnerability there?
- Why wasn't it patched?
- Why wasn't the alert seen?
- Why is no one answering the SOC phone after 3 PM?

Use techniques like:

- Fishbone diagrams
- Fault tree analysis
- Log correlation

The point? Get past the symptom (e.g., "We got hacked") to the underlying disease (e.g., "No patching process + alert fatigue = incident").

4. What Worked? What Didn't?

Call out wins and fails like a game show host:

Good:

- Quick alert from EDR
- Network segmentation limited lateral movement
- Comms team had templates ready

Bad:

- Took 2 hours to find the right incident handler
- PR released a statement with the wrong timestamp (oops)
- Logs were overwritten before analysis

Be honest. This is where real maturity happens.

5. Document Lessons Learned

Create a list of concrete lessons:

- "EDR alerts should trigger auto-ticketing."
- "Backups need to be tested monthly."
- "We need better training on phishing."
- "We should probably not let interns manage firewall rules."

Add supporting evidence, screenshots, logs — and keep it professional but real.

Bonus: Include quotes from responders. ("I realized halfway through the incident that we didn't even have a runbook for SQL injection...")

6. Action Plan for Improvement

Here's where you commit to change (and not just put it on the shelf).

A good action plan includes:

- What needs to be done
- Who owns it
- When it's due
- Status updates and follow-up checks

Examples:

Action	Owner	Deadline	Status
Create patch management policy	IT Security Lead	Aug 15	In progress
Train staff on phishing awareness	HR + Security	July 20	Scheduled
Update incident response runbooks	SOC Manager	Aug 5	Not started

7. Share the Report (Wisely)

Tailor versions of your report for different audiences:

- Executives want impact, cost, timeline, and future readiness
- Tech teams want root cause, timeline, logs, and action items
- Legal/compliance want documentation and regulatory impact

Keep it secure — you don't want your "We got breached because..." story becoming front-page news.

Continuous Improvement Loop

Once the review is done, don't just move on. Feed your learnings into:

- Updated IR playbooks
- New training content
- Security architecture improvements
- Policy updates
- Simulation planning

Pro tip: Run tabletop exercises based on your own incidents — not just generic "nation-state attack" scenarios. Nothing says "real-world practice" like reliving your own chaos.

Real-World Wrap-Up: The Pizza Breach

A startup got breached through a phishing email offering free pizza. Yes, seriously. The attacker got into their dev environment, altered code, and introduced a backdoor.

Post-incident review revealed:

- No MFA on Git repos
- No alert on sudden IP change
- The dev team had no training on phishing
- Improvements included:
- Mandatory MFA
- Security onboarding for new devs
- Simulated phishing campaigns (ironically, starting with free pizza)

Lesson learned: Free pizza isn't always free.

Final Thoughts: Reflect or Repeat

The point of a post-incident review isn't just to wrap up paperwork — it's to build a stronger, smarter defense and make your organization more resilient over time.

"Incidents happen. But improvement is a choice."

So sit down, grab some coffee (and maybe tissues), relive the pain — and walk out with wisdom.

Chapter 7: Third-Party and Supply Chain Risk Management

Your vendors are like in-laws: you didn't pick them, but their behavior can cause you endless headaches. Supply chain attacks? Yeah, those are the party crashers of cybersecurity. It's not enough to lock your own doors—you've got to make sure your neighbors aren't letting the burglars in.

This chapter explores how to identify and manage risks that arise from external partners, vendors, and service providers. You'll learn how to conduct third-party risk assessments, establish security baselines in contracts, and monitor vendors continuously to safeguard the entire supply chain. It's an essential piece of holistic cyber risk management.

7.1 Evaluating Vendor Security Posture

"Trusting a vendor without vetting their security is like giving your house key to a raccoon in a tuxedo — looks cute, but you'll probably regret it."

So, your business runs on a delightful cocktail of third-party services — cloud platforms, payment gateways, HR software, that one random tool marketing insisted on because it had "the best fonts."

But here's the deal: Your cybersecurity is only as strong as your weakest vendor. And if you're not evaluating their security posture, you might as well be leaving the back door wide open and yelling "Come on in!"

In this chapter, we're diving into how to properly assess the security of your vendors — before they become your biggest risk.

Why Vendor Security Matters

A quick reality check:

- **Target's 2013 data breach?** Caused by a third-party HVAC vendor.
- **SolarWinds?** A supply chain attack through software updates.
- **MOVEit breaches in 2023?** Yep, third-party file transfer software.

Third-party = third-party risk. And if they touch your systems, data, or customers, they must be scrutinized like an ex's new partner on Instagram.

What Is a Vendor's Security Posture?

It's the overall strength of a vendor's:

- Technical defenses
- Security policies
- Risk management practices
- Response capabilities

In plain speak: Are they cyber-clueless, or do they actually know what a firewall is (and no, not the one in Game of Thrones)?

Step-by-Step: How to Evaluate a Vendor's Security

Let's walk through it like the cautious cyber-sleuth you are:

1. Define the Scope of the Relationship

Before grilling a vendor, figure out:

- What systems will they access?
- Will they process/store customer or employee data?
- Are they handling regulated info (PII, PHI, cardholder data)?
- Is this a long-term partnership or a one-time thing?

The higher the access and sensitivity, the deeper your evaluation should go.

2. Initial Risk Assessment

Segment vendors based on criticality and risk exposure:

- **High-risk:** Cloud storage, payroll platforms, SaaS tools tied to production
- **Medium-risk:** Marketing software, analytics tools
- **Low-risk:** Snacks supplier (unless they have access to your building network, and then...wow, you've got bigger problems)

Use a risk matrix or tiering model to prioritize who gets the full inspection.

3. Security Questionnaires and Due Diligence

Ah yes, the famous vendor security questionnaire — loved by auditors, feared by salespeople. It typically includes questions about:

- Data encryption (at rest and in transit)
- Access controls and MFA
- Network segmentation
- Incident response processes
- Security audits and certifications (SOC 2, ISO 27001)
- Vulnerability management
- Secure software development lifecycle (SDLC)

Warning: Don't just accept "Yes" as an answer. Ask for evidence — reports, screenshots, or documentation. If their response smells like "copy-paste from ChatGPT," dig deeper. (Hey, even I can't secure your server for you!)

4. Request Security Certifications & Audit Reports

Certifications are not a golden ticket, but they do show a commitment to security. Ask for:

- SOC 2 Type II
- ISO 27001

- PCI-DSS (if handling card data)
- HIPAA (if handling health data)

Also request:

- Penetration test summaries
- Third-party audit results
- Internal risk assessments (if they're open to sharing)

Pro tip: Watch out for expired certs or vague promises like "we're working toward compliance" — it's like saying, "I plan to go to the gym... someday."

5. Evaluate Data Handling and Privacy Practices

Especially if the vendor processes personal or sensitive data, ask:

- **Where is the data stored?** (Geolocation matters for GDPR and other laws)
- **Who has access to it?**
- **Do they have a data retention policy?**
- **What happens to data after termination?**

For regulated industries, demand Data Processing Agreements (DPAs) and Privacy Impact Assessments (PIAs).

6. Review Their Incident Response Readiness

This one's big. Ask:

- Do you have an IR plan?
- Who do we contact during an incident?
- Will you notify us of a breach involving our data — and how quickly?

Time is everything. If they wait 30 days to tell you about a breach while your customers are already tweeting angrily... yeah, not ideal.

7. Ongoing Monitoring and Reassessment

One-and-done doesn't cut it.

- Review vendors annually or biannually — especially high-risk ones
- Monitor news and threat feeds for vendor breaches

Use tools like:

- SecurityScorecard
- BitSight
- UpGuard
- RiskRecon

If your vendor pops up in a ransomware gang's leak list — you wanna know before your CISO does.

Contractual Protections (AKA "You Breach It, You Bought It")

Bake security into the contract. Clauses should include:

- Right to audit
- Required security controls
- Breach notification timelines
- Data destruction on contract end
- Liability and indemnification terms
- Sub-processor disclosures

Get Legal involved — no, seriously. A solid contract is your best fallback when "good faith" turns into "good luck."

Build a Third-Party Risk Management Program

Don't just wing it every time you get a new vendor. Formalize your process:

- Create a Vendor Risk Register
- Establish tiered vendor levels
- Use standard templates and questionnaires
- Automate where possible
- Make security reviews part of procurement

This way, nobody accidentally signs off on a new tool that "connects directly to prod" without a single security check.

Real-World Tale: The Social Media Scheduler Snafu

A company outsourced social media management to a vendor using a cheap, no-name scheduler. The vendor got phished. The attacker took over the scheduler — and began posting weird crypto ads from the company's Twitter account.

Why?

- No MFA on the scheduler
- No vendor review before onboarding
- No contractual obligation to notify breaches

Lesson? Even seemingly "low-risk" vendors can trash your reputation in minutes.

Final Thoughts: Vendors Are Partners — So Pick Wisely

"Choosing vendors without reviewing their security is like marrying someone after one great date and zero background checks. Sure, they brought flowers... but do they even lock their doors?"

So:

- Ask hard questions
- Dig for proof
- Document everything
- Build a repeatable process

A secure vendor is a good partner. An insecure one? Well, they just became your next incident response exercise.

7.2 Third-Party Risk Assessments

"Third parties: because who doesn't love giving strangers a backstage pass to your network?"

In the world of cybersecurity, third-party risk assessments are like checking your roommate's friends before they crash at your place for the weekend. Just because you lock your doors and don't microwave metal doesn't mean your guest isn't going to burn the house down.

Third-party vendors, partners, suppliers, and service providers are critical to operations — but also represent a juicy attack surface for cybercriminals. From cloud platforms to consultants, everyone you do business with can introduce risk. And if you're not proactively evaluating that risk, you're basically playing cyber Jenga... blindfolded.

So let's unpack how to perform a smart, structured, and slightly suspicious third-party risk assessment. (Spoiler alert: trust is earned, not assumed.)

What Is a Third-Party Risk Assessment?

A third-party risk assessment is the process of evaluating the cybersecurity posture, practices, and risks associated with external entities that your organization works with.

In plain English:

You're checking if your vendors are likely to leak your data, go rogue, or accidentally get hacked by clicking on "Hot Singles Near You."

This involves assessing how they:

- Handle sensitive data
- Secure their networks and infrastructure
- Respond to incidents
- Comply with laws and regulations

Why It Matters

Still wondering why you should care? Let's hit you with a few fun facts:

- Over 60% of data breaches are linked to third parties.
- Regulatory frameworks like GDPR, HIPAA, and CCPA require due diligence on vendors.
- Your customers don't care who caused the breach — they'll still blame you.

Bottom line: You can outsource services, but you can't outsource accountability.

How to Perform a Third-Party Risk Assessment

Alright, time to put on your cyber detective hat and start assessing like a pro.

1. Inventory All Third Parties

You can't assess what you don't know exists. Start by compiling a complete list of third-party relationships, including:

- Cloud services (AWS, Azure, GCP)
- SaaS platforms (CRM, HR, finance)
- Managed service providers (MSPs)
- Contractors and freelancers
- Supply chain partners
- That guy Steve hired to "optimize the Wi-Fi" once

Make sure to include shadow IT — the tools employees adopt without formal approval (you know it's happening).

2. Classify Vendors by Risk

Not all vendors are created equal. Some handle sensitive data or have deep access to your systems. Others just deliver snacks (and hopefully not ransomware).

Use a risk tiering model:

Tier	Description	Example
High	Access to critical systems or sensitive data	Payroll provider, cloud hosting
Medium	Indirect access or moderate data	Marketing automation, CRM
Low	No system/data access	Office supply vendor, food caterer

Prioritize deeper assessments for high-risk vendors. Nobody wants to spend 3 hours auditing a donut delivery app (unless...).

3. Send Security Questionnaires

Now it's time to probe! Security questionnaires help you understand a vendor's controls, policies, and mindset.

Typical topics include:

- Authentication (MFA? Password policies?)
- Encryption (at rest and in transit)
- Data retention and deletion
- Backup and disaster recovery
- Security awareness training

- Incident response plans
- Pen testing and vulnerability management
- Regulatory compliance (SOC 2, ISO 27001, etc.)

Tip: Use tools like OneTrust, Whistic, or SecurityScorecard to streamline this process and reduce back-and-forth emails.

4. Validate Their Responses

Don't just take their word for it. Always validate with:

- SOC 2 or ISO audit reports
- Pen test results (even just summaries)
- Certificates and attestations
- Sample policies or redacted logs
- Privacy impact assessments (PIAs)
- Data processing agreements (DPAs)

Red flag: If a vendor is "not allowed" to share anything, you're either dealing with extreme secrecy or... a serious problem.

5. Assess Legal and Regulatory Risk

Make sure your vendor complies with relevant laws:

- **GDPR** (for EU personal data)
- **CCPA/CPRA** (California)
- **HIPAA** (health info)
- **PCI-DSS** (card payments)

Review contracts and ensure they:

- Outline breach notification responsibilities
- Include data handling and deletion clauses
- Assign liability clearly
- Allow audits (yes, this matters)

Bonus tip: Always get legal involved — this is their jam.

6. Perform Continuous Monitoring

The assessment doesn't stop once you sign the contract. Vendors change, grow, get acquired — or get breached.

Use tools to monitor:

- Security ratings (via BitSight, RiskRecon, etc.)
- News alerts and breach databases
- Public disclosure filings
- Dark web mentions (just in case your vendor's credentials are making the rounds)

Reassess vendors annually (at minimum), or more frequently for high-risk services.

7. Define Exit Strategy and Offboarding Process

Eventually, vendors change or relationships end. When that happens, you need to:

- Terminate access (VPN, SSO, databases)
- Retrieve or destroy data
- Remove from network maps and asset lists
- Confirm compliance via termination checklists

You ghost a vendor without offboarding properly, and boom — that ghost just hacked your SharePoint.

Common Pitfalls to Avoid

Let's laugh at our shared pain (and learn from it):

- Skipping assessments for "trusted" partners
- Accepting vague answers like "we follow best practices"
- Failing to reassess vendors after major incidents
- Overloading vendors with 500-question forms for low-risk services
- Ignoring subcontractors (your vendor's vendor can mess you up too)

Real-World Story: The Fancy PR Firm Fumble

A company hired a PR firm for a product launch. Seemed harmless, right?

Wrong.

The firm had access to internal calendars, contacts, and press materials — and their system got phished. Result? Pre-release product info leaked. A competing firm beat them to market.

Lesson: Even low-tech, non-IT vendors can become vectors. Always evaluate. Always monitor.

Final Thoughts: Trust, but Verify (Then Re-Verify)

"When it comes to third parties, paranoia isn't just healthy — it's policy."

You're not just protecting your organization — you're protecting your customers, data, and reputation. That makes third-party risk assessment a must-have, not a "nice to have."

So get nosy. Ask questions. Demand evidence. Build a program.

Because when your vendor gets breached, your inbox fills up with your customers asking you what happened.

7.3 Contractual Safeguards and SLAs

"*Ah, contracts — the grown-up version of pinky promises, but with more lawyers and fewer glitter pens.*"

Let's get real: you can throw all the security questionnaires, risk assessments, and vendor vetting in the world at a third party — but if your contract doesn't have solid safeguards and crystal-clear expectations, you're just hoping for the best. And hope, my friend, is not a strategy. Especially not in cybersecurity.

That's where Contractual Safeguards and Service Level Agreements (SLAs) come in. Think of them as your cyber prenup — defining what each party is responsible for, how data is handled, and what happens if things go sideways.

Let's break it down. And don't worry, we'll keep the legalese to a minimum. No law degree required — just a good sense of paranoia and a healthy respect for fine print.

What Are Contractual Safeguards?

Contractual safeguards are legally binding clauses you put into your contracts with third parties to protect your organization from cybersecurity risks. These clauses define:

- Security expectations
- Data protection obligations
- Incident response timelines
- Legal liability and indemnification
- Privacy compliance
- Termination conditions

Basically, they answer the important questions:

- "What happens if your vendor messes up?"
- "Who's responsible for what?"
- "How quickly do they have to fix it?"
- "Who pays when the digital stuff hits the fan?"

Why SLAs Matter in Cybersecurity

SLAs — Service Level Agreements — are part of the contract where you set performance expectations. In the cybersecurity world, that can mean:

- System uptime guarantees

- Response time for incidents or vulnerabilities
- Patch deployment timelines
- Breach notification timeframes
- Backup frequency and data restoration speeds

It's like a "cyber performance report card" — and if the vendor doesn't make the grade, you've got the power to enforce penalties or corrective actions.

Without SLAs, you're just hoping they feel like doing the right thing when things go wrong.

Must-Have Contractual Safeguards (No, Seriously)

Here are the clauses that should be in every vendor contract worth its weight in firewalls:

1. Data Security Requirements

Spell it out in detail:

- Encryption standards (AES-256? TLS 1.3?)
- Access controls (MFA required? Role-based access?)
- Secure development practices (DevSecOps, SDLC)
- Logging and monitoring expectations

Pro Tip: Refer to accepted frameworks (NIST, ISO 27001) to avoid reinventing the wheel.

2. Breach Notification Obligations

Time is everything. Make it crystal clear:

- How soon must the vendor notify you after a breach?
- Who do they contact on your team?
- What info must they include (affected systems, data types, mitigation steps)?

Industry standard: 24–72 hours. Anything longer = red flag.

3. Right to Audit and Assess

You need the legal right to:

- Conduct periodic audits
- Review security documentation
- Validate compliance

Even if you don't audit everyone, this clause keeps vendors honest. Like putting up a "Smile, you're on camera" sign — you may not be watching, but they'll act like you are.

4. Data Ownership and Handling

Who owns the data? (Hint: it should be you.)

Make sure the contract covers:

- Data usage limits (no selling, sharing, or "anonymized marketing" shenanigans)
- Data retention and deletion policies
- Secure return or destruction upon termination

Ghosting a vendor is fine. Letting them ghost your customer data? Not so much.

5. Subcontractor/Sub-processor Approval

Vendors love vendors — but that doesn't mean you should trust their friends.

Include a clause requiring:

- Disclosure of all subcontractors handling your data
- Right to approve or reject those subs
- Flow-down of the same security obligations

You don't want to vet one vendor only for them to hand your data to their sketchy cousin Doug.

6. Regulatory Compliance and Standards

Make sure the contract requires compliance with relevant laws and frameworks:

- GDPR, CCPA, HIPAA, PCI-DSS
- SOC 2, ISO 27001, NIST 800-53

Don't just say "must comply with applicable laws." Be specific. If it's not in writing, it doesn't exist — at least not when the lawyers show up.

7. Indemnification and Liability Limits

If a vendor's mistake leads to a breach, who pays?

- **Indemnification:** Vendor agrees to cover costs/damages related to security incidents caused by their negligence.
- **Liability limits:** Cap the vendor's financial responsibility — or negotiate uncapped liability for breaches or gross negligence.

Bonus clause: Make sure your cyber insurance doesn't exclude claims caused by third parties.

8. Termination for Security Failures

Include the right to terminate the contract if:

- The vendor experiences repeated or serious security failures
- There's a breach and inadequate response
- They can't meet your compliance requirements

You've got to be able to cut ties — fast — if your vendor turns into a liability.

What to Include in SLAs (Cyber Edition)

Your Service Level Agreements should be as sharp as your firewall. Here's what to lock in:

SLA Area	Recommended Metric
Uptime	99.9%+ availability
Incident Response	< 2 hours to acknowledge, < 24 hours to respond
Breach Notification	24–72 hours max
Patch Deployment	Critical patches applied within 7 days
Backup Frequency	Daily backups with weekly full backups
Recovery Time Objective (RTO)	≤ 24 hours
Recovery Point Objective (RPO)	≤ 1 hour for critical data

Tip: Tie missed SLAs to financial penalties or service credits. Suddenly vendors become a lot more punctual.

Work with Legal, Not Against Them

Contracts can be intimidating. That's why your legal team exists — bring them in early. Work together to:

- Use standardized security addendums
- Define "reasonable" security measures clearly
- Map contract clauses to risk tiers (more strict for higher-risk vendors)

Build a template you can reuse for consistency. If every contract is a custom legal jigsaw puzzle, your procurement team is going to revolt.

Make It Living, Not Static

Review your contracts regularly:

- Did the vendor introduce new services or access points?

- Did regulations change?
- Was there a recent security incident?

Your contracts need to grow with the relationship — like a cactus that occasionally bites back.

Real World Oops: The SLA-Free File Share Fail

One company outsourced their document sharing system to a third-party vendor. They had no SLA for uptime or breach response. Naturally, the vendor went down for four days after a ransomware attack — and took the company's entire deal pipeline with it.

With no SLA, no indemnity, and no breach clause, the company was stuck watching leads die on the vine while the vendor scrambled.

Lesson: If it's not in writing, it's not enforceable. ◈

Final Thoughts: Lawyers, Limits, and Lockdowns

"A well-written contract won't prevent a breach — but it will make sure someone else foots the bill."

Cyber risk management isn't just about firewalls and forensics — it's about making sure your legal safety net is bulletproof. With solid safeguards and SLAs, you're setting boundaries, defining expectations, and holding vendors accountable — all before disaster strikes.

So next time someone says, "Oh, we don't need to worry, we trust this vendor," gently remind them:

Trust is cool. Contracts are cooler.

7.4 Managing Supply Chain Attacks

"*Supply chains: where one vendor clicking a cat meme can take down an entire global enterprise.*"

Ah, the supply chain. A beautiful symphony of manufacturers, software providers, logistics companies, third-party APIs, coffee machine vendors (yep, even them) — all working together in glorious, interconnected harmony. Until... BOOM

Suddenly, that tiny vendor with one overworked IT guy just became Patient Zero in your corporate cyber nightmare. Welcome to the wild world of supply chain attacks — where attackers don't knock on the front door, they just hitch a ride in the back of someone else's delivery truck.

So, pull up a chair, grab your risk register, and let's dive into how to manage these sneaky, spaghetti-like cyber threats from your extended digital family.

What Is a Supply Chain Attack?

In simple terms:

A supply chain attack is when an attacker targets your organization by compromising a third-party service, software, or partner that you trust and use.

Instead of hacking you directly, they hack the folks you rely on — because it's often easier. It's like robbing a bank by breaking into the janitor's closet first.

Examples include:

- Software updates injected with malware
- Compromised firmware in hardware before it even ships
- Trusted vendors leaking credentials or data
- API integrations acting like insecure backdoors
- Open-source packages that get hijacked or poisoned

If you've heard of SolarWinds, Kaseya, or Log4j, you already know supply chain attacks aren't rare unicorns. They're real. They're brutal. And they're growing faster than a TikTok trend.

Why Supply Chain Attacks Are So Dangerous

Let's break it down:

- **Stealthy:** These attacks often go undetected for months.
- **High trust** = high access: Vendors already have privileged access.
- **Scale:** One attack can impact hundreds or thousands of downstream organizations.

- **Patch delays:** You can't fix what someone else broke — and they're often slow to react.
- **Shared responsibility confusion:** Everyone points fingers while attackers point commands.

In short: They hit hard, hide well, and spread fast. Like glitter at a craft party.

How to Manage Supply Chain Attacks

Alright, here comes the good part — what you can actually do about it. Spoiler: there's no silver bullet, but there is a smart strategy.

1. Map Your Supply Chain

You can't protect what you can't see.

Start by identifying:

- All third-party software dependencies (yes, even the tiny browser plugin Steve installed)
- Hardware vendors and manufacturers
- Service providers (cloud, MSPs, SaaS)
- API integrations and external code libraries
- Partners with network access (even that one weird B2B portal from 2009)

Create a supply chain dependency map — think of it like Google Maps for risk.

2. Risk-Tier Your Vendors

Not all supply chain partners are equal. Use a risk-based approach to classify them:

- **High risk:** Access to sensitive data, core infrastructure, critical services
- **Medium risk:** Bsiness-impacting but not mission-critical
- **Low risk:** No access to internal systems or sensitive data

This helps you prioritize your efforts and not burn out assessing your snack delivery service (unless it runs on a vulnerable Linux kernel — you never know).

3. Assess Third-Party Security Posture

Conduct formal assessments and reviews, especially for high-risk vendors:

- Security questionnaires
- SOC 2 / ISO 27001 reports
- Penetration test summaries

- Software bill of materials (SBOMs)
- Secure coding practices and DevSecOps

Want to go pro? Ask them if they monitor their own supply chain too. Yup, it's turtles all the way down.

4. Use Zero Trust Architecture

Zero Trust isn't just a buzzword — it's tailor-made for managing supply chain risk.

- **Don't automatically trust any user, device, or service** — verify everything.
- **Apply least privilege access** — vendors only get access to what they need.
- **Use network segmentation** — isolate third-party connections.
- **Monitor all traffic continuously** — especially from vendor tools or apps.

Remember: "Assume breach" is the mindset. "Trust but verify" is the mood.

5. Secure Your Software Development Lifecycle (SDLC)

If you build software, you ARE the supply chain.

Protect it by:

- Scanning for vulnerable libraries (use SCA tools)
- Signing code and verifying signatures
- Using tamper-proof CI/CD pipelines
- Implementing change management controls
- Monitoring for dependency confusion and typosquatting (yep, it's a thing)

And please... no downloading code from random GitHub gists and pasting it into production.

6. Monitor for Indicators of Compromise (IoCs)

Set up active monitoring for:

- Anomalous activity from vendor IPs or user accounts
- Unexpected API calls or changes in behavior
- Command-and-control traffic
- Known IoCs tied to supply chain malware campaigns

Tools like SIEMs, XDR, and threat intel feeds are your best friends here.

7. Define a Response Plan for Supply Chain Attacks

Your incident response plan needs to specifically account for third-party breaches.

It should include:

- Pre-identified contacts for critical vendors
- Contractual obligations (see previous chapter)
- Internal escalation paths
- Isolation strategies
- Communication templates (for regulators, customers, press)

Because when your vendor gets hacked, your customers will still expect you to have answers.

8. Demand Transparency and Accountability

Encourage or require:

- Software Bills of Materials (SBOMs)
- Public vulnerability disclosures
- Secure development certifications
- Prompt notification of any security incidents

And yes — if a vendor refuses to be transparent, it's okay to say "no thanks." Or at least "not until you fix that gaping security hole you're pretending doesn't exist."

Real-World Wake-Up Call: SolarWinds

The SolarWinds Orion hack is a case study in how a single compromised software update turned into a global catastrophe. Attackers inserted malware into a routine software patch, which got pushed to 18,000+ customers — including U.S. government agencies.

That's like updating your calendar app and accidentally inviting an APT to your board meeting.

Lesson? Every line of code you inherit from someone else is a potential trojan horse — treat it accordingly.

Final Thoughts: Your Risk Is Only as Strong as Their Password

"Managing supply chain attacks isn't about paranoia — it's about realism. And maybe a little healthy paranoia too."

You can't build a fortress and leave the back gate wide open for your vendors. Managing supply chain attacks means acknowledging that your digital ecosystem is bigger than your org chart — and that attackers love the weakest link.

So assess. Monitor. Contract. Control. Isolate. Respond.

Oh, and one last thing...

If your vendor's idea of security is "we use really strong Wi-Fi passwords," it might be time to re-evaluate that relationship.

7.5 Tools for Continuous Vendor Monitoring

"Remember that time you trusted a vendor blindly and everything went just fine? Yeah... me neither."

You've assessed the vendor. You've read the contract. You even smiled and nodded through their PowerPoint full of "state-of-the-art encryption." But here's the thing: cybersecurity is a marathon, not a checkbox.

That means ongoing, real-time, and automated monitoring of your vendors. Because a vendor that was secure 6 months ago might be compromised today — and you don't want to find out after the headlines hit.

Welcome to the world of Continuous Vendor Monitoring. Not as sexy as AI or blockchain, but arguably way more important.

So grab your coffee (or something stronger), and let's unpack the tools that help you keep a digital eye on your extended enterprise 24/7/365.

Why Continuous Monitoring?

Vendor assessments are often point-in-time snapshots — like judging someone's hygiene based on a single shower.

But things change. Patches get missed. Employees leave. Breaches happen. Without ongoing visibility, you're flying blind.

Continuous monitoring solves that by giving you alerts, trends, and real-time intel when your vendors:

- Appear in a new breach dump
- Lose a critical certificate
- Change their domain config
- Miss patching known vulnerabilities
- Have exposed cloud storage (hello, S3 buckets!)

It's like having a security camera on your third-party ecosystem. And yes, the footage gets spicy.

Categories of Monitoring Tools (And Why They Matter)

Let's break down the toolbox. Most mature programs use a combo of these tools — not just one magic solution.

1. Third-Party Risk Intelligence Platforms

Think of these as the big dogs of vendor monitoring — continuously scanning the public internet and dark web for risks tied to your vendors.

Popular Tools:

- SecurityScorecard

- BitSight
- RiskRecon (by Mastercard)
- UpGuard
- Black Kite

What they do:

- Give vendors a security "credit score"
- Monitor for vulnerabilities, misconfigurations, expired certs
- Check for exposed services, ports, domains
- Alert you when something changes (or breaks)

Pro tip: These tools can also track your vendors' vendors (aka your 4th party risk — because why stop at three?)

2. GRC & TPRM Platforms (Governance, Risk & Compliance)

These are full platforms that combine assessment, workflow, and monitoring — like the Swiss Army knife of vendor oversight.

Examples:

- OneTrust
- Archer (RSA)
- LogicGate
- ProcessUnity
- ServiceNow VRM

They help you:

- Manage questionnaires and audits
- Track remediation workflows
- Connect risks to business impact
- Monitor ongoing vendor status

Best for: large orgs with tons of vendors and compliance requirements.

3. Attack Surface Management (ASM)

These tools don't just monitor vendors — they monitor you too. And that's important because attackers often pivot between partners.

Examples:

- Palo Alto Cortex Xpanse
- Randori
- CyCognito
- Rezilion

They:

- Continuously scan your external-facing assets
- Identify shadow IT or forgotten vendor tools
- Catch misconfigured domains, APIs, SSL issues
- Help you visualize your third-party risk exposure

Bonus: ASM tools often find stuff even your vendors forgot they were running.

4. Cloud Security Posture Monitoring (CSPM)

If your vendors live in the cloud (and who doesn't these days?), you'll want CSPM visibility — especially for IaaS, SaaS, and PaaS environments.

Examples:

- Prisma Cloud (by Palo Alto)
- Wiz
- Orca Security
- Lacework

They can alert you to:

- Misconfigured S3 buckets
- Over-permissioned IAM roles
- Unpatched containers
- Exposed databases

Because it turns out "someone else's computer" can be just as vulnerable as yours.

5. Dark Web Monitoring

Even if your vendor swears they're secure, their credentials might be chilling on a dark web forum right now.

Examples:

- SpyCloud
- Constella Intelligence
- Recorded Future
- IntSights

They alert you to:

- Credential dumps
- Stolen API keys or tokens
- Fraudulent domains or impersonation
- Threat actor chatter mentioning your vendors

Creepy? Yes. Necessary? Also yes.

How to Use These Tools Effectively

Having tools is great. Using them smartly is better. Here's how to squeeze every drop of value:

Set Risk Thresholds

Don't treat all vendors the same. Customize alert thresholds based on:

- Criticality of vendor
- Data sensitivity
- Regulatory exposure
- Integration depth

A payment processor slipping on patching?

Your digital whiteboard app with 3 users down for an hour? Maybe just a slack message.

Integrate Alerts into Your IR and SOC

Make sure alerts from vendor monitoring tools go to the right teams:

- Security Operations Center (SOC)
- Incident Response (IR)

- GRC/Compliance
- Procurement (yep, they need to know when it's time to say goodbye)

Real-time alerts are only useful if they're seen in real time.

Automate Playbooks

When a vendor's rating drops or a new vulnerability is found:

- Trigger reassessment workflows
- Open tickets for remediation
- Notify the vendor
- Escalate internally if SLA or contract terms are violated

With good automation, your TPRM team won't burn out by month three.

Periodically Reassess and Adjust

The threat landscape changes. So should your monitoring strategy.

- Add new tools as you grow
- Swap out underperformers
- Monitor tool accuracy with internal testing

Like any good security program — this ain't "set it and forget it."

Real World Oops: The "We Thought They Were Secure" Vendor

A healthcare company trusted a long-term transcription vendor. No continuous monitoring. All looked well.

Until one day, a researcher found 10,000+ patient records publicly accessible due to a misconfigured AWS bucket. No alert. No warning. Just... disaster.

It turns out the vendor had moved to a new cloud setup. Nobody noticed. Nobody checked.

Lesson: Past performance ≠ present security. Stay in the loop, or be left in the breach.

Final Thoughts: Tools Are Great, But Don't Lose the Plot

"You don't need all the tools — just the right ones. And a team that actually looks at the alerts."

Continuous vendor monitoring doesn't mean turning into a digital stalker. It means being proactive, informed, and prepared. With the right tools, you get peace of mind — or at least fewer surprises during board meetings.

So embrace the dashboards. Love the alerts. Trust, but verify. And if a vendor goes radio silent every time something weird shows up... maybe they're not the partner you thought they were.

Chapter 8: Emerging Threats and Future Challenges

The future is here—and it's trying to hack you. AI-powered phishing scams, quantum computer-powered decryption, and toaster ovens with WiFi. What a time to be alive (and paranoid)! Let's take a peek into tomorrow's threat landscape and try not to scream into the cloud.

This chapter examines the latest trends in cybersecurity and emerging threats that organizations must prepare for. Topics include artificial intelligence, quantum computing, cloud security, Internet of Things (IoT), and critical infrastructure protection. Understanding these evolving risks is key to developing adaptive and forward-looking cyber strategies.

8.1 AI and Machine Learning in Cybersecurity

"First AI came for your chess game... then your writing... and now it's defending your network like a digital ninja with a PhD."

Alright, let's talk about the cool kids in cybersecurity town: Artificial Intelligence (AI) and Machine Learning (ML). If cybersecurity were a superhero movie, AI would be that mysterious new character who shows up in the third act, knows kung-fu, speaks every language, and hacks bad guys with a smirk.

But it's not all sci-fi and sentient firewalls. AI and ML are now deeply integrated into how we detect, prevent, and respond to threats — often faster than a human analyst could blink, or at least faster than Greg in IT finishing his third coffee.

Let's unpack how AI/ML are reshaping cyber risk management — and how to use them without becoming Skynet.

What Exactly Is AI and ML (Without the Buzzword Fluff)?

- **Artificial Intelligence (AI):** A system or machine that mimics human cognitive functions — learning, reasoning, problem-solving.
- **Machine Learning (ML):** A subset of AI that enables systems to learn from data and improve over time without being explicitly programmed.

In human terms: AI is the genius intern that never sleeps and keeps getting smarter — ML is how it trains itself to become your company's top analyst in a week.

Why AI/ML Is a Game-Changer in Cybersecurity

Traditional cybersecurity tools rely on signatures and rules — kind of like "if A happens, do B." But cybercriminals don't always play by the rules. They constantly adapt, morph, and innovate (annoyingly fast).

That's where AI/ML shine:

- They don't need predefined rules
- They detect patterns humans can't see
- They learn from new attacks in real-time
- They can spot anomalies instead of just known threats

Basically, AI doesn't just look for bad guys — it figures out what normal looks like, and screams when something weird happens.

Where AI/ML Are Used in Cybersecurity

1. Threat Detection & Anomaly Hunting

AI/ML algorithms analyze terabytes of logs and traffic to identify suspicious behaviors — like:

- A user logging in from Nigeria at 2 a.m.
- A process executing a base64-encoded PowerShell script
- A fridge in the office suddenly scanning the entire network (yes, that happened)

Popular tools:

- CrowdStrike Falcon
- Darktrace
- Microsoft Defender for Endpoint
- Cisco SecureX

They spot stealthy attacks that signature-based tools would miss — like zero-days, polymorphic malware, and insider threats.

2. Behavioral Analytics (UEBA)

User and Entity Behavior Analytics (UEBA) uses AI to build a "normal" profile for each user/device — and then flags anything offbeat.

Examples:

- Alice in HR never uses FTP... until today?
- Bob normally logs in from LA... now he's in Beijing and Boston simultaneously? Uh oh.

UEBA reduces false positives and helps focus attention on real threats.

3. Automated Threat Response

AI doesn't just detect — it can also react:

- Quarantining endpoints
- Blocking IPs in real-time
- Isolating compromised accounts
- Kicking off incident response workflows

SOAR (Security Orchestration, Automation, and Response) platforms like Splunk Phantom, Cortex XSOAR, or Swimlane often use ML-driven decisions to act faster than any human could type "sudo shutdown."

Think: Robotic bouncer at your digital nightclub.

4. Email and Phishing Protection

Phishing has leveled up. No more broken English and sketchy links — today's phishing emails look cleaner than corporate newsletters.

AI helps by:

- Detecting subtle spoofing techniques
- Understanding context and intent in emails
- Spotting impersonation attempts

Tools like Abnormal Security, Microsoft Defender for Office 365, and Cofense are all using ML models to keep inboxes safe from disaster.

5. Malware Detection & Sandboxing

Traditional AV needs a known signature to stop malware. AI-powered AV doesn't.

Instead, ML models look at:

- File behavior
- Execution flow
- Entropy levels (yep, that's a thing)

Even if the malware has never been seen before, AI might still flag it based on how it acts. Think of it like watching someone wear a ski mask and walk into a bank — you don't need to wait for the robbery to start.

6. Fraud and Identity Protection

Banks, e-commerce platforms, and even social networks use AI/ML to:

- Detect account takeovers
- Monitor transactions for fraud patterns
- Prevent identity spoofing
- Analyze login attempts and behavior

Ever got a message saying "We noticed suspicious activity on your account"? That's probably a ML model working behind the scenes.

Limitations (Because No, It's Not Magic)

Let's kill the hype for a second. AI isn't a silver bullet. It has challenges too:

- **False positives:** Early models can cry wolf — a lot.

- **Training data:** If the model isn't trained well, it's as useful as a chocolate firewall.
- **Adversarial AI:** Hackers are now using AI to trick AI. Yep.
- **Bias:** If you train an AI on biased data, it'll carry that bias into decisions. Not ideal for security.

You still need human analysts, threat hunters, and IR teams — AI is the assistant, not the commander (yet...).

Best Practices for Using AI in Cyber Risk Management

Here's how to make the most of AI without tripping over it:

- **Know the use case** — Don't buy AI just to say you have AI.
- **Start small** — Use AI for one function (e.g., phishing protection), then expand.
- **Feed it good data** — Clean, quality data is the fuel for good AI.
- **Validate performance** — Regularly test the AI against new threats.
- **Combine AI with human expertise** — AI finds anomalies. Humans provide context.

AI's job isn't to replace your SOC — it's to make it smarter, faster, and less reliant on caffeine and miracles.

Final Thoughts: Use the Bots... Before the Bots Use You

"AI won't save your company alone — but it might save your analysts from drowning in alerts."

The future of cybersecurity isn't about man or machine — it's man and machine. With the sheer volume and complexity of modern threats, automation and intelligence aren't just nice-to-haves — they're survival tools.

So embrace the algorithms. Train them. Tune them. And let them handle the noisy stuff so your humans can focus on strategy, response, and asking the real questions... like "Who left the firewall wide open again?"

8.2 Quantum Computing and Cryptographic Risk

"Remember when your biggest worry was someone stealing your Netflix password? Yeah... those were the good old days. Welcome to the quantum era."

Okay, let's get quantum.

Imagine a computer so powerful it could unravel today's encryption like peeling a banana — in milliseconds. That's not just a plot twist from a sci-fi flick — it's the real, looming threat of quantum computing. And while quantum machines haven't broken the internet yet, they've got traditional cryptography sweating bullets.

This chapter's about why quantum computing matters to cybersecurity, what cryptographic risks it brings, and how to prepare without completely panicking.

What Is Quantum Computing? (Without Melting Your Brain)

Let's keep this simple, promise.

- Traditional computers use bits (0s and 1s).
- Quantum computers use qubits, which can be 0, 1, or both at the same time (thanks, Schrödinger).
- This superposition and entanglement allow quantum computers to process a gazillion possibilities all at once.

What does that mean in practice?

It means certain problems — like factoring huge numbers or simulating molecules — can be solved exponentially faster than with classical computers.

TL;DR: Where traditional computers would take years, a quantum computer could crack it in seconds. And yes, that includes the stuff protecting your online bank.

The Cryptographic Panic Button: Why We're Worried

Today's digital security depends heavily on asymmetric encryption — the kind where there's a public key and a private key. Think:

- RSA
- ECC (Elliptic Curve Cryptography)
- DH (Diffie-Hellman)
- These rely on mathematical problems that are hard to solve with current tech.

But along comes quantum computing, wielding something called Shor's Algorithm — a quantum algorithm that can break RSA and ECC like they're puzzles from a cereal box.

What's at Risk?

- HTTPS (yep, that little lock icon in your browser)
- VPNs and secure tunnels
- Digital signatures and certificates
- Blockchain security (especially older ones)
- Your encrypted backups and sensitive data

So yes — everything.

When Will Quantum Be a Real Threat?

Great question. Here's the consensus:

- **Current status:** Still in experimental stages. Quantum supremacy has been achieved in lab conditions, but not for real-world crypto-busting... yet.
- **Experts predict:** Practical quantum computers that can break RSA-2048 may appear by 2030–2040.

And yes, that feels far off — until you realize attackers can steal encrypted data today, store it, and decrypt it later when quantum becomes available. This is called:

Harvest Now, Decrypt Later (HNDL)

A future hacker classic.

Enter: Post-Quantum Cryptography (PQC)

If quantum computers threaten traditional encryption, then post-quantum cryptography is the superhero we need.

These are cryptographic algorithms designed to resist quantum attacks, using math problems that even a quantum computer can't solve (or not in this century, at least).

Types of PQC Algorithms

- Lattice-based cryptography (NTRU, Kyber)
- Hash-based signatures
- Multivariate polynomial cryptography
- Code-based cryptography

Some of these are battle-tested, while others are still being poked at by cryptographers (aka professional code-breakers with too much coffee).

NIST to the Rescue

The National Institute of Standards and Technology (NIST) launched a global competition to develop and standardize quantum-resistant algorithms.

As of now:

- Finalists include Kyber (for encryption) and Dilithium (for digital signatures).
- Standardization is expected to be completed soon.
- Once finalized, vendors and governments will start integrating them into real-world systems.

So yes, the quantum cavalry is assembling.

Real-World Example: Google, IBM & Quantum Labs

Tech giants like Google and IBM are already building quantum machines and testing PQC integration.

- Google achieved "quantum supremacy" in 2019 — their quantum computer solved a problem in 200 seconds that would take classical supercomputers thousands of years.
- IBM, Amazon, and Microsoft have all launched Quantum-as-a-Service platforms. Yes, quantum in the cloud. Because why not?

Meanwhile, companies like Cloudflare, Mozilla, and Signal have been quietly experimenting with post-quantum encryption in browsers and messengers.

What You Can Do (Without Building a Quantum Lab in Your Garage)

You don't need to panic. But you do need to prepare. Here's how to start:

1. Inventory Your Cryptography

Find out:

- What crypto algorithms you're using
- Where they're implemented (apps, hardware, communications)
- How long the data needs to remain confidential (Hint: anything >5 years = vulnerable)

Call it a "crypto census" — and no, it won't be fun. But it's essential.

2. Plan for Crypto-Agility

Crypto-agility = the ability to switch algorithms without breaking everything.

Make sure your systems:

- Support multiple encryption algorithms

- Allow for updates and patches easily
- Use modular crypto libraries

This way, when post-quantum standards are finalized, you can upgrade smoothly instead of screaming into the void.

3. Watch NIST and Industry Updates

Keep an eye on:

- NIST PQC announcements
- Vendor roadmaps (e.g., AWS, Microsoft, Cisco)
- Regulatory guidance from agencies like NSA, ENISA, or CISA

In the future, compliance will likely require PQC, so don't be the last one to the party.

4. Talk to Your Vendors (Yes, All of Them)

Start asking:

- *"Are you PQC-ready?"*
- *"What's your quantum-safe roadmap?"*
- *"How do you handle crypto upgrades?"*

You'll quickly find out who's serious about security... and who's still stuck in 2012.

Final Thoughts: The Quantum Storm Is Coming — But You've Got Time (Kind Of)

"Quantum computers might not break your encryption tomorrow, but they've definitely RSVP'd to the party."

Quantum risk is real, but it's not about doomsday — it's about preparation. The organizations that win the future will be the ones who:

- Know their crypto landscape
- Build agility into their systems
- Embrace change early

So don't wait until your firewall starts humming weird frequencies or the AI assistant starts quoting Schrödinger.

Start planning now, be adaptable, and remember: the future is quantum... but your security doesn't have to collapse like a probability wave.

8.3 Cloud and Container Security Risks

"Remember when servers were actual boxes you could kick in a data center? Now everything's floating in a magical cloud—and containers are multiplying like rabbits on caffeine."

Let's be honest—moving to the cloud was supposed to make life easier, right? Fewer physical servers, elastic scalability, and the joy of saying "our infrastructure is fully containerized" in meetings to sound cool.

But with great flexibility comes... a giant pile of new risks. The cloud and container ecosystems are powerful, but they're also like leaving your house with 14 doors and only locking 3 of them.

This chapter breaks down the risks, gotchas, and real-world messes that come with securing cloud environments and containerized applications. Buckle up, it's about to get cloudy with a chance of misconfigurations.

What's the Big Deal with Cloud Security?

Cloud computing isn't just "someone else's computer." It's a highly dynamic, scalable, distributed infrastructure where:

- Apps can spin up in seconds
- Data moves faster than gossip in a Slack channel
- Services talk to each other like a high-speed whisper network

But all that automation, abstraction, and convenience also makes it really easy to screw up — and really hard to notice when something goes wrong.

Key Challenges:

- Shared responsibility model confusion
- Misconfigurations galore
- Identity sprawl
- Shadow IT ("Wait, who launched this AWS account?!")

Top Cloud Security Risks

Let's unpack the usual suspects:

1. Misconfigured Cloud Storage Buckets

You've seen the headlines:

"Company X leaks 80 million records due to open S3 bucket."

It's one of the oldest tricks in the hacker book: scanning for exposed cloud storage buckets. Common issues include:

- Public access enabled unintentionally
- No encryption at rest
- No logging or monitoring

It's the cloud version of leaving your front door open and posting "we're out of town" on social media.

2. Identity and Access Management (IAM) Mayhem

In the cloud, IAM is the gatekeeper. Screw it up, and attackers can:

- Escalate privileges
- Access sensitive data
- Launch other services

Risks include:

- Overly permissive roles (e.g., *:*)
- Lack of MFA
- Dormant accounts with high privileges

Always follow the Principle of Least Privilege (PoLP)—not "let Bob from marketing spin up EC2 instances just because he asked nicely."

3. Inadequate Visibility

Unlike on-prem environments, where you can (mostly) see everything, cloud environments are:

- **Ephemeral** (things come and go)
- **Dynamic** (autoscaling, microservices)
- **Multi-layered** (infra + platform + app)

This makes logging, monitoring, and incident detection a massive headache if you don't have the right tools and architecture.

Remember: You can't protect what you can't see.

4. Insecure APIs and Endpoints

APIs are the lifeblood of the cloud. But when poorly secured, they're also the weak spots attackers love.

Risks include:

- Lack of rate limiting

- Weak authentication
- Leaky endpoints exposing sensitive data

You can secure your infrastructure perfectly—and still be owned by one unprotected REST endpoint. REST in peace.

Container Security Risks

Containers are fast, light, and efficient—but also stack up their own list of security concerns like it's Black Friday.

Here's what to watch out for:

1. Insecure Images

Containers are built from base images—sort of like meal kits. If the base image has expired software or vulnerabilities, every container you spin up inherits that risk.

Common issues:

- Pulling images from untrusted registries
- Outdated packages
- Hidden backdoors in public images (yep, that happens)

Pro tip: Always use trusted, signed images and scan them like they owe you money.

2. Weak Isolation

Containers share the same kernel. That's great for efficiency, not so great for security. If a container escapes its sandbox, it might:

- Access the host OS
- Interfere with other containers
- Compromise the entire node

Think of it like apartment tenants sharing the same floor—and one of them decides to knock a hole through the wall.

3. Secrets in the Image or Code

Storing secrets (API keys, passwords, tokens) in environment variables, config files, or—brace yourself—hardcoded in source code is a disaster waiting to happen.

There's an entire subclass of attacks focused on finding these secrets inside container images or CI/CD pipelines.

Use secret management tools, not .env files that end up on GitHub.

4. Unsecured CI/CD Pipelines

Your containers are only as secure as the pipeline that builds them. Risks include:

- Insecure GitHub repos
- Compromised build tools
- Lack of code review
- Supply chain attacks

CI/CD is supposed to automate deployment—not automate breaches.

Best Practices for Cloud & Container Security

You don't have to abandon the cloud or ditch containers — just get smart about how you secure them.

Here's your cheat sheet:

For Cloud:

- Enable MFA on all accounts
- Use role-based access control (RBAC)
- Encrypt data at rest and in transit
- Audit logs and set alerts (use AWS CloudTrail, GCP Cloud Audit Logs, Azure Monitor)
- Automate misconfig detection with tools like Wiz, Prisma Cloud, or ScoutSuite

For Containers:

- Scan container images regularly (Trivy, Anchore, Clair)
- Use minimal base images (e.g., Alpine)
- Run containers as non-root users
- Use runtime protection (e.g., Falco, AppArmor, SELinux)
- Isolate workloads using namespaces and cgroups

Bonus tip: Have a beer with your DevOps team. These folks are your new best friends.

Tools That Make Life Easier

Purpose	Tools
Cloud Security Posture Mgmt (CSPM)	Wiz, Orca, Prisma Cloud, AWS Security Hub
Container Scanning	Trivy, Clair, Snyk
Secrets Mgmt	HashiCorp Vault, AWS Secrets Manager, Doppler
IAM Auditing	Prowler, IAM Access Analyzer
Runtime Threat Detection	Falco, Sysdig Secure

Use them. Love them. Thank them later.

Final Thoughts: Cloud's Not Insecure—Just Misunderstood

"The cloud is secure. It's your configuration that isn't." — every security engineer ever

Cloud and containers aren't inherently dangerous. But when we rush into them without planning, we create environments that are flexible and fragile.

So lock down your S3 buckets, secure your containers, and for the love of cyber hygiene, stop hardcoding credentials in GitHub.

8.4 IoT and Industrial Control Systems (ICS) Threats

"Once upon a time, your toaster just toasted. Now it's part of a Wi-Fi mesh network with root access and a grudge. Welcome to the Internet of (Insecure) Things."

IoT and ICS devices are like the party guests that show up early, connect to every Bluetooth speaker, and leave the front door open. They're helpful, smart, and everywhere—but from a cybersecurity perspective, they're also a giant pain in the firewall.

Whether you're securing a smart fridge or protecting an oil refinery's control systems, the threats facing these devices are very real—and in some cases, life-threatening. In this chapter, we'll break down the security risks, real-world attacks, and how you can defend your networks before your lightbulbs start phishing employees.

What Are IoT and ICS, Anyway?

Let's clarify who's who in this increasingly cyber-connected world:

IoT (Internet of Things)

These are your everyday smart devices:

- Smart thermostats
- Voice assistants (yes, Alexa's listening)
- Security cameras
- Wearables, sensors, vending machines... you name it

IoT is about convenience and automation, often found in homes, offices, hospitals, and cities.

ICS (Industrial Control Systems)

This includes devices that manage:

- Power grids
- Water treatment plants
- Manufacturing systems
- Oil and gas pipelines

ICS is about safety, precision, and real-world consequences—we're talking explosions, outages, and national security implications.

IoT makes life comfy. ICS keeps the lights on and planes flying. Both, unfortunately, often come with cybersecurity nightmares.

Why Are They So Risky?

Let's break it down:

1. Lack of Built-In Security

Many IoT/ICS devices were built for function, not security. Think:

- Default credentials (admin:admin)
- Unpatched firmware
- No encryption
- No logging

It's like buying a new safe with a sticky note on it that says "the key is under the mat."

2. Long Lifespans, Slow Updates

ICS equipment can run for decades, and patching isn't always feasible. Downtime? That's a no-go when your job is keeping nuclear reactors running.

IoT? Some manufacturers abandon updates after 6 months. It's the cybersecurity equivalent of a deadbeat dad.

3. Poor Network Segmentation

Many organizations plug IoT and ICS into the same flat network as everything else:

Smart thermostat → Corporate Wi-Fi → File server

Without segmentation, a vulnerability in one coffee machine could become the gateway to your entire infrastructure. (And yes, it's happened.)

4. Authentication? What's That?

Insecure APIs, hardcoded credentials, or no authentication at all? Check, check, and check.

Many IoT devices assume "you're on the network, so you're trusted." That's like letting someone into your house because they look like a pizza delivery guy.

Real-World Attacks That Should Terrify You (Just a Little)

The Mirai Botnet (2016)

This legendary malware turned insecure IoT devices (like routers and IP cameras) into a giant botnet that took down Twitter, Netflix, GitHub, and more.

Cause? Default login credentials.

Effect? Massive DDoS attack.

Moral of the story? Change your damn passwords.

Stuxnet (2010)

The mother of all ICS attacks. Allegedly created by nation-states, this worm specifically targeted Iranian nuclear centrifuges, silently sabotaging them.

Stuxnet didn't steal data—it broke stuff. Physically.

It proved that malware could cause real-world destruction.

Oldsmar Water Plant Hack (2021)

An attacker remotely accessed a Florida water treatment system and tried to increase sodium hydroxide (lye) levels to dangerous amounts.

Luckily, a human operator noticed and corrected it.

But the attacker got in via TeamViewer with poor security.

Defending IoT and ICS Systems

Okay, let's not just panic—let's get proactive. Here's what smart defenders are doing:

1. Change Default Credentials (No, Really)

This is step one, day one, always. If your device ships with a default login, change it immediately. Use a password manager to keep things organized and strong.

2. Patch and Update (When Possible)

- Regularly check for firmware and software updates.
- Enable auto-update if available.
- For ICS, follow strict change control policies and test updates before deployment.

Yes, patching ICS isn't easy. But leaving known vulnerabilities is like sending an open invite to every hacker on the dark web.

3. Network Segmentation Is Your Best Friend

Separate IoT and ICS devices from your core networks using:

- VLANs
- Firewalls
- Zero Trust models

If your smart fridge can talk to your payroll system, you've already lost.

4. Monitor Everything

Use intrusion detection systems (IDS), anomaly detection, and SIEM platforms to:

- Monitor traffic from IoT and ICS devices
- Alert on suspicious behaviors (e.g., device suddenly reaching out to a server in North Korea)

You can't fight what you can't see.

5. Conduct Risk Assessments and Pen Tests

Test your environment like a hacker would:

- Look for exposed ports
- Run vulnerability scans
- Simulate breaches in a controlled way

You don't want to find out about a flaw when someone else already has.

6. Use Device Management Solutions

Solutions like:

- Microsoft Defender for IoT
- AWS IoT Device Defender
- Nozomi Networks
- Claroty for ICS

These platforms can help you manage, monitor, and secure your endpoints, especially at scale.

Checklist: IoT/ICS Security Essentials

- Inventory all devices
- Change default credentials
- Patch/firmware update policy
- Segmentation from critical systems
- Enable logging and monitoring
- Limit internet exposure
- Disable unused ports and protocols
- Conduct regular audits
- Have an incident response plan tailored for IoT/ICS

Final Thoughts: The Internet of Things Is Also the Internet of Threats

"If it's smart enough to connect to the internet, it's smart enough to be hacked."

IoT and ICS are incredible technologies that make modern life possible—from smart homes to entire power grids. But the same features that make them convenient also make them vulnerable.

So whether you're managing smart lights or gas turbines, the lesson is the same:

Visibility, segmentation, and good ol' cyber hygiene go a long way.

And maybe—just maybe—don't give your fish tank IoT access to your guest Wi-Fi. (Yes, that's also happened. In Vegas. At a casino.)

8.5 Cybersecurity in a Globalized Digital Economy

"Remember when the biggest cross-border risk was a bad fax? Now a teen in another hemisphere can drain your crypto wallet while eating cereal. Welcome to the global stage."

The digital economy is like one massive online party where everyone's invited—companies, consumers, cloud providers, even your grandma's smart doorbell. And when everything is connected, so are the risks. What starts as a cyber hiccup in one country can ripple into a full-blown meltdown in another.

So in this chapter, we're zooming out—way out—to look at the cybersecurity challenges of a globally connected, always-on, always-online economy. Grab your passport (and a firewall); we're going international.

What Is the Global Digital Economy?

Imagine the global economy doing a backflip into cyberspace. That's the digital economy:

- Cross-border e-commerce
- Remote workforces
- Global supply chains
- Cloud computing
- Digital payments and cryptocurrency

All powered by networks, data, and applications that live... basically everywhere. But that interconnectivity means cyber risks don't respect borders, business hours, or bureaucracies.

Your cloud provider might be in the U.S., your dev team in India, your data hosted in Germany, and your threat actor sipping espresso in Italy while breaching your network.

Key Cybersecurity Challenges in a Borderless World

1. Varying Data Privacy Laws

One of the biggest headaches for global businesses: trying to comply with a dozen different privacy frameworks at once.

- **GDPR (EU):** Strict data processing & consent rules
- **CCPA (California):** Consumer rights on data
- **PDPA (Singapore),** LGPD (Brazil), PIPEDA (Canada)... the list goes on

It's like a cyber game of "Twister," and one wrong move could mean fines, lawsuits, or angry regulators.

2. Skills Gap on a Global Scale

Cyber talent is in short supply everywhere. Companies are going global not just for business, but for staffing their SOCs (Security Operations Centers).

But:

- Training levels vary wildly
- Language and cultural barriers affect response
- Not every region has strong cyber education or regulation

Result? Inconsistent defense. It's like having locks on some doors and duct tape on others.

3. Cybercrime Is Global, Too

Bad actors don't need visas. Ransomware gangs, phishing groups, and nation-state APTs (Advanced Persistent Threats) operate from anywhere:

- Ransomware-as-a-Service (RaaS) groups offer support in multiple languages
- Crypto payments let attackers go borderless and anonymous
- Tactics are shared across forums and Telegram faster than memes

It's truly a cyber United Nations, except everyone's armed and no one's agreeing on anything.

4. Supply Chain Vulnerabilities

You may trust your vendors, but do you trust their vendors?

Think of:

- Software libraries (e.g., Log4j)
- Cloud providers and their configurations
- Hardware sourced internationally

One insecure third-party can bring down an entire digital operation. This is how one dodgy component can compromise 1,000 companies overnight. (Thanks, SolarWinds.)

5. Infrastructure Disparities

Not every country has:

- Reliable encryption laws
- Updated infrastructure
- Fast patching cycles
- Strong internet governance

This creates weak spots in the global security fabric—ideal places for threat actors to hide, launch attacks, or store stolen data.

It's like playing cyber Jenga—pull the wrong piece from the global stack and watch it fall.

So What Can We Do About It?

We can't build a giant cyber wall (sorry, firewalls don't count), but we can take steps to secure global operations.

1. Embrace Global Security Standards

Adopt and align with internationally recognized frameworks:

- **ISO/IEC 27001** – Gold standard for global ISMS (Information Security Management Systems)
- **NIST CSF** – Widely respected and flexible framework
- **CIS Controls** – Practical, prioritized, and language-neutral

Pro tip: Use these as your "security lingua franca."

2. Perform Country-Specific Risk Assessments

Not every country is equal when it comes to cyber risk. Evaluate:

- Local threat actors
- Regulatory environments
- Critical infrastructure maturity

Tailor your cybersecurity strategy per region. Think of it like sunscreen—you need more in sunny places.

3. Monitor International Threat Intel

Follow threat intelligence from:

- Global CERTs (Computer Emergency Response Teams)
- Interpol & Europol cyber crime units
- Open-source threat feeds

Stay updated on malware trends, phishing campaigns, and geopolitical events that could impact your systems—even if they're happening halfway across the world.

4. Collaborate Across Borders

Cybersecurity isn't a solo sport—it's a global team game:

- Join Information Sharing and Analysis Centers (ISACs)

- Participate in industry-specific forums
- Work with law enforcement when appropriate

Remember, the enemy already collaborates. Why shouldn't we?

5. Encrypt, Segment, and Zero Trust It All

Universal defense tactics:

- Encrypt all sensitive data (in transit and at rest)
- Use Zero Trust Architecture—trust nothing by default
- Segment networks so an attack in one region doesn't spill into another

And hey, maybe stop putting production and dev environments in the same cloud account across continents. (Looking at you, Chad in IT.)

Real-World Example: Maersk & NotPetya

In 2017, Maersk—a global shipping giant—was collateral damage in the NotPetya ransomware attack (originally aimed at Ukraine). The result?

- Their entire network went down
- 49,000 devices had to be reinstalled
- Estimated losses: $200–300 million

This showed that a single attack targeting a foreign country could ripple into multinational companies that had nothing to do with the conflict.

Lesson? In a globalized economy, no one is a bystander. You're either prepared... or vulnerable.

Final Thoughts: Local Actions, Global Repercussions

"The butterfly effect is real in cybersecurity. One missed patch in Prague can ruin a merger in Miami."

The global digital economy is fast, innovative, and limitless—but it's also risky, complex, and constantly targeted. Cybersecurity professionals now need to think not just locally, but globally.

So yes, defend your perimeter. But also:

- Know your international laws
- Vet your vendors
- Monitor the world stage

And update your dang firewall rules—before someone from halfway across the globe rewrites them for you.

Chapter 9: Metrics, KPIs, and Reporting for Risk Management

You ever try to explain a firewall to your CEO? It's like describing a unicorn with a PhD. That's where metrics come in. Numbers don't lie, and they help translate geek speak into boardroom applause (or at least less confused blinking).

This chapter addresses the importance of quantifying cybersecurity performance through metrics and key performance indicators (KPIs). You'll learn how to design meaningful dashboards, generate executive reports, and quantify the value of cybersecurity initiatives through risk-based metrics. This data-driven approach enables strategic decision-making at every level of an organization.

9.1 Defining Security Metrics and KPIs

"Metrics: because 'I think we're secure' isn't a great strategy—unless your business model involves hoping really hard."

Ever walked into a boardroom and tried to explain cyber risk using only passion, gut feelings, and vibes? Yeah, that doesn't fly. In today's world, if you can't measure it, you can't manage it—and you definitely can't convince your CFO it matters.

That's where security metrics and KPIs (Key Performance Indicators) step in. They give structure to the chaos and help translate "cyber-ese" into business-speak. Let's explore how you can choose and use the right ones to show progress, find weaknesses, and justify that shiny new EDR tool you've been eyeing.

What Are Security Metrics and KPIs?

Let's get one thing straight:

- Security Metrics = Raw data or measurements
- → "We had 87 phishing attempts last month."
- Security KPIs = Strategic indicators tied to goals
- → "We reduced phishing-related incidents by 20% in Q2."

In simple terms, metrics tell you what's happening, while KPIs tell you if it's working.

Why Metrics Matter (Yes, Even to Non-Tech People)

Good metrics help you:

- Track security posture over time
- Show ROI on tools, staff, and training
- Spot trends and potential gaps
- Support compliance and audits
- Justify funding (hello, budget season)

Imagine telling leadership:

"Thanks to our 24/7 threat hunting team, we reduced mean time to detect (MTTD) by 30%!"

That gets attention.

"I think we're doing okay."

That gets you cut from the budget.

Characteristics of Good Security Metrics

Not all metrics are created equal. Great ones are:

Quality	What It Means
Relevant	Tied to business or security goals
Actionable	Helps you decide what to do next
Repeatable	Consistently measurable over time
Accurate	Based on reliable data
Understandable	You don't need a PhD in cryptography to explain it

Bad metrics? They're like calories on a salad when you added a pound of ranch—technically there, but misleading and unhelpful.

COMMON SECURITY METRICS (aka the Hits)

Here's your starter pack of metrics that matter:

Detection & Response

- MTTD (Mean Time to Detect) – How long it takes to spot threats
- MTTR (Mean Time to Respond) – How long to fix/contain them
- Number of incidents detected per month
- Percentage of false positives in alerts

Why it matters: The faster you detect and respond, the less damage you take.

Phishing & User Behavior

- Phishing click-through rate
- Number of users reporting phishing attempts
- Security awareness training completion rate

Why it matters: Your users are your frontline—and sometimes your weakest link. These metrics show if training works or if Dave from Accounting needs another refresher.

Access and Identity

- Percentage of users with MFA enabled
- Number of privileged accounts created or removed

- Inactive accounts older than 90 days

Why it matters: If your identity systems aren't tight, attackers walk right in—no brute force needed.

Patch and Vulnerability Management

- Average time to patch (by severity)
- Number of known vulnerabilities unpatched
- Percentage of critical systems fully patched

Why it matters: Unpatched systems are hacker gold mines. Track this like your career depends on it—because it might.

Risk and Compliance

- Number of audit findings (open vs resolved)
- Compliance scores (e.g., NIST CSF, ISO 27001)
- Third-party vendor risk assessments completed

Why it matters: Whether it's regulators or customers, someone's watching—and they like metrics.

Pro Tips for Defining Your KPIs

Choosing KPIs is like choosing your Netflix watchlist: don't go overboard, and make sure each one has a purpose.

Here's how to pick the good ones:

1. Align with Business Goals

If your org's top priority is uptime and customer trust, your KPIs should reflect availability and incident impact, not just firewall stats.

2. Start Small and Scale

Begin with 5–10 KPIs. Track them well. Then add more. Don't try to boil the internet in one quarter.

3. Review Regularly

Metrics should evolve with threats and business changes. That KPI from 2018 about "number of floppy disks encrypted" might not be too helpful now.

4. Tailor for Your Audience

- **C-suite:** Business impact, financial exposure, trends
- **Security teams:** Technical depth, detection gaps, control performance
- **Operations:** Patch timelines, response speed, system uptime

No one wants to sit through a 40-slide SIEM export. (Except maybe your intern. Maybe.)

Example KPI Dashboard (Simplified)

KPI	Target	Current Value	Trend
Phishing Click Rate	< 5%	3.2%	Decreasing
Mean Time to Detect (MTTD)	< 24 hours	19 hours	Stable
Critical Patch Time (avg)	< 7 days	12 days	Needs Work
MFA Adoption	100%	93%	Improving
Vendor Risk Assessments Completed	100% of vendors	75%	Moderate

You don't need flashy dashboards (though they help). You need clarity and consistency.

What to Avoid: The Vanity Metric Trap

Some metrics sound impressive but don't help you act. These include:

- Total number of alerts (unless tied to false positives)
- "Blocked threats" (without context)
- Number of antivirus scans run

They're like flexing at the gym but skipping leg day. Don't do it.

Final Thoughts: Measure What Matters

"Security metrics are your compass. Without them, you're just sailing in the fog hoping not to crash."

The beauty of well-defined metrics is that they help security teams speak the language of impact, improvement, and investment—instead of panic, jargon, and "we'll get back to you."

So whether you're tracking patch velocity or user awareness, remember: clear, relevant metrics are what separate mature security programs from the ones that only think they're secure.

And hey, if you can get your phishing report rate up and your false positives down, go ahead—brag a little. You earned it.

9.2 Dashboards for Real-Time Monitoring

"Ah, dashboards—because staring into the abyss of logs and alerts without visuals is like trying to find Waldo in binary."

Let's be real: cybersecurity produces a lot of data. Logs, alerts, anomalies, user behaviors, threat intel—if it had calories, we'd all be in excellent shape.

But data without visibility is just chaos in disguise. That's where real-time dashboards come into play. They don't just look cool on a giant SOC monitor wall (although they do). They let you monitor, detect, respond, and brag to your boss—all in real time.

So, let's roll up our sleeves and explore how to build and use dashboards that don't just show stuff—but show the right stuff.

What Is a Real-Time Security Dashboard?

A real-time dashboard is a visual interface that displays live (or nearly live) security data. Think of it as the cyber weather radar for your organization.

Good dashboards:

- Aggregate data from multiple sources (SIEMs, firewalls, EDR, IDS, cloud platforms)
- Provide a bird's-eye view and drill-down capabilities
- Let you spot patterns, anomalies, and "oh no" moments

TL;DR: Dashboards help you see the cyber storm before it hits your servers.

Why Dashboards Matter

Because "we'll check the logs later" is not a viable incident response strategy. Dashboards help by:

- Improving situational awareness
- Reducing time to detect/respond
- Supporting incident triage
- Empowering non-tech stakeholders with digestible info
- Making your SOC look like NASA

Also, let's be honest—no one wants to present 500 rows of CSV data at a board meeting.

Must-Have Dashboard Widgets (a.k.a. The Greatest Hits)

Let's break down the MVP lineup for a real-time security dashboard:

1. Active Alerts by Severity

- Critical, High, Medium, Low
- Color-coded for easy "oh crap" moments

Why? Helps prioritize what to tackle first—don't treat a brute-force attempt like a misplaced USB stick.

2. Top Threats / Attack Types

- Ransomware, phishing, brute-force, malware, etc.
- Trends over time

Why? Knowing the how helps improve the how-to-stop-it.

3. Geo-Location of Threats

- Visual heatmap or globe

Why? "Why are we getting login attempts from North Korea at 2 AM?" is a good question to be asking.

4. User Behavior Anomalies

- Logins at weird hours
- Impossible travel
- Sudden privilege changes

Why? Users gonna user—but dashboards let you catch when they suddenly go rogue.

5. Endpoint Status Summary

- Devices out-of-date
- Offline endpoints
- Active threats

Why? You can't protect what you can't see. Don't let Steve's unpatched laptop sink the ship.

6. Patch & Vulnerability Status

- Patch compliance rates
- Top 10 unpatched CVEs

Why? Vulnerabilities don't get bored and leave—they wait patiently.

7. Email Threats Detected

- Phishing attempts blocked
- Malicious attachments
- User-reported emails

Why? Because email is still the #1 threat vector. And Karen from HR just clicked another "invoice."

8. Network Traffic Anomalies

- Spikes in outbound traffic
- Data exfiltration alerts
- Suspicious ports/protocols

Why? Exfil is the new exploit—catch it before your data's halfway to a dark web auction.

9. Trends Over Time

- Incidents by day/week/month
- Progress on KPIs

Why? Dashboards aren't just for now—they help show if things are getting better (or scarier).

Pro Tips for Building Effective Dashboards

Now that you know what to show, let's talk how to show it.

1. Customize by Audience

- **Executives:** Business impact, compliance, financial exposure
- **SOC Analysts:** Real-time alerts, threat indicators, endpoint status
- **IT Ops:** Patch levels, system health, config changes

Different eyes = different dashboards

2. Keep It Clean and Actionable

Don't clutter the screen with every single metric. This isn't a Vegas slot machine.

Stick to:

- Clear visuals (graphs, gauges, heatmaps)
- Fewer words, more signals

Actionable insights > vanity metrics

3. Integrate Everything You Can

Your dashboard should pull from:

- **SIEM** (e.g., Splunk, Sentinel, QRadar)
- **Endpoint Protection** (e.g., CrowdStrike, Defender)
- **Network Tools** (e.g., Zeek, Suricata)
- **Cloud Services** (AWS GuardDuty, Azure Security Center, etc.)

Threat Intel feeds

Basically, if it beeps, logs, or screams—connect it.

4. Automate Alerts & Escalations

Use thresholds and triggers to:

- Email the SOC when critical alerts spike
- Open tickets in your IR platform
- Slap your on-call analyst via Slack (figuratively... usually)

Let your dashboard work for you, not the other way around.

Tools to Build Killer Dashboards

You've got choices—here are some popular options:

Tool	Good For
Splunk	Massive enterprise data, custom viz
Elastic Stack	Flexible, open-source, powerful
Microsoft Sentinel	Seamless Azure + built-in dashboards
Datadog	Hybrid cloud environments
Grafana + Loki	Custom dashboards, lightweight setups
Kibana	Part of ELK, great visual interface

Also—some SIEMs come with prebuilt dashboards. Don't reinvent the wheel unless the wheel's flat.

Dashboard Fails to Avoid

- Too much red. If everything's an emergency, nothing is.

- Ignoring context. A blocked threat isn't always a real threat.
- Static data. If it's not refreshing in real-time, it's just a glorified PowerPoint.

Bonus fail: using Comic Sans on a ransomware dashboard. Just... no.

Final Thoughts: Dashboards That Actually Defend

"Dashboards aren't just cyber eye candy. They're your mission control panel. Use them wisely."

A well-designed real-time dashboard is your early warning system, your strategy tracker, and your cyber confidence booster all rolled into one. It gives you control in the chaos and lets you act before the breach hits the fan.

So invest the time to build dashboards that inform, alert, and drive action—not just look pretty in a screenshot.

And remember: the best dashboard isn't the flashiest—it's the one that gets you to sleep at night. Or at least lets you spot what's keeping you up.

9.3 Reporting to Executives and Boards

> *"Explaining cybersecurity to the board is like describing a ransomware attack to your grandma: less jargon, more impact, and absolutely no acronyms without translation."*

Alright, time to talk about one of the most high-stakes performance art pieces in cybersecurity: reporting to executives and the board. These are the people who approve budgets, set priorities, and—let's be honest—don't care how many packets were dropped by the firewall unless it directly affects revenue, reputation, or regulation.

If you walk in talking like a SOC console ("...and then our IDS triggered a high-fidelity IOC based on lateral SMB traffic..."), you'll lose them faster than a weak password at a hacker convention.

This chapter is your playbook to translate security into business, drive alignment, and actually get things done (like getting that SIEM upgrade you've been begging for since last fiscal year).

The Goal: Storytelling with a Security Backbone

Reporting isn't about showing everything you did—it's about showing the risks you're managing, the progress you're making, and why it all matters to the business.

Remember: The board wants answers to three big questions:

- Are we at risk?
- Are we improving?
- Are we spending wisely?

If your reports don't touch on those, you're just another line in the PowerPoint graveyard.

Know Your Audience (And Their Attention Span)

Boards and execs aren't ignoring you—they're just being pulled in 17 directions at once. So respect their time by tailoring your message.

Executives (CFO, COO, CMO, etc.)

- **Focus on:** financial exposure, operational impact, brand protection
- **Speak in:** risk, ROI, compliance, cost savings

Board Members

- **Focus on:** governance, oversight, long-term risk
- **Speak in:** risk trends, accountability, business continuity, reputation

CISOs (if you're reporting to your peers)

- **Focus on:** strategic progress, metrics, gaps
- **Speak in:** maturity models, KPI trends, threat intelligence

Pro Tip: No one wants to hear about port scans unless the scans lead to breach risk and impact revenue.

What to Include in a Good Executive Report

Let's break down the ingredients of a tasty executive-friendly report.

1. Executive Summary

- TL;DR of current risk landscape
- Highlights of wins and concerns

"We've reduced phishing incidents by 35%, but patch compliance dipped due to a vendor issue."

Make it readable in 30 seconds. Bonus points for a graphic or traffic-light system.

2. Current Risk Posture

- High-level view of threat landscape
- Top 3 risks to the business right now
- Comparison to previous quarter

Include visuals like:

- Heatmaps
- Risk scoring charts
- Risk register trends

Example: "Credential stuffing remains the #1 threat vector due to exposed credentials from third-party leaks."

3. Key Performance Indicators (KPIs)

Pick 5–8 that matter. Examples:

- Mean Time to Detect (MTTD)
- Mean Time to Respond (MTTR)
- Phishing click rate
- Patch compliance % (especially for critical systems)
- MFA adoption rate

Avoid overwhelming them with 35 KPIs. That's how you end up with glazed eyes and delayed funding.

4. Incident Summary (If Any)

- Brief overview of major security incidents
- What was the impact?
- What was the response?
- Lessons learned and improvements made

No need to list every blocked port scan. Stick to what made a dent or could have.

5. Compliance and Legal Exposure

- Status of key frameworks: GDPR, HIPAA, CCPA, PCI-DSS, etc.
- Upcoming audits or recent findings
- Potential fines or gaps that need attention

You're not just defending data—you're defending from lawsuits and regulators too.

6. Strategic Investments and Roadmap

- Where are you spending?
- What's the ROI or expected outcome?
- What do you need more of (tools, people, training)?

This is your chance to make the business case for that new XDR tool or cloud security upgrade.

Think like a CFO: "We're spending $150K to reduce breach likelihood by 60% and cut downtime risk."

Presentation Tips: Turning Tech into Talk

Even the best data will flop if delivered poorly. Here's how to nail the delivery:

Tell a Story

Frame your message like a movie:

- What's the threat?
- What's the potential damage?
- What are we doing about it?
- What do we still need?

Narratives stick better than spreadsheets.

Use Visuals, Not Text Walls

- **Graphs** > Paragraphs
- **Traffic lights** > Bullet points
- **Dashboards** > Data dumps

Just remember: make visuals simple, clean, and self-explanatory. If it takes 10 minutes to explain one chart, it's not executive-ready.

Respect the Clock

If you've got 15 minutes, don't build a 40-slide deck. Prioritize your message, and be ready for Q&A on business impact, not just tech.

Speak the Language of Risk

Tech: "We've had 500 brute-force login attempts."

Exec-speak: "We blocked an attempt to compromise privileged accounts, which could have led to data exfiltration and compliance violations."

Bonus Section: Quick Wins that Impress Boards

Here are a few executive crowd-pleasers:

- "We achieved a 90% MFA adoption rate across the enterprise."
- "No data breaches this quarter. All security SLAs met."
- "We aligned our risk framework to NIST CSF and passed a third-party audit."
- "Our phishing test click rate dropped from 20% to 4%."

Bonus: Add a graph with a downward trend for threat incidents. It makes people happy.

Tools to Make Reporting Easier

Skip the manual effort. These tools help automate or enhance executive reporting:

Tool	Best For
Power BI / Tableau	Beautiful, dynamic dashboards
Splunk Enterprise	Data aggregation + executive views
ServiceNow GRC	Risk and compliance dashboards
Excel + Canva (yes, really)	Quick visuals for lean teams

Just make sure your data is accurate. Nothing kills credibility like reporting a "0% phishing rate" the day after the CEO gets phished.

Final Thoughts: Talk Risk, Not Routers

"If the board walks away knowing which firewall vendor you use, you've missed the point. If they walk away knowing how you're protecting the business, you nailed it."

Reporting to execs and boards isn't about dumbing down the tech—it's about translating its value. You're not just protecting systems; you're protecting revenue, reputation, and resilience.

So next time you're crafting that report, ditch the acronyms, use clean visuals, speak in risk, and show how your work moves the needle.

And hey—throw in one cyber joke at the end. If you can make a board member chuckle, they'll probably remember your budget request.

9.4 ROI of Cybersecurity Investments

"Ah yes, the age-old debate: 'Why spend money to not get hacked?' It's like asking why you pay for brakes if you've never crashed."

Cybersecurity is one of the few departments in an organization where success often looks like... nothing happened. No breach, no incident, no front-page headline with your company's name next to "leak" or "ransomware."

But convincing execs and bean counters to spend on something they don't see is tough. That's where Return on Investment (ROI) for cybersecurity comes in. It helps shift the perception from "cost center" to "business enabler."

Let's break down how to measure it, communicate it, and—yes—even brag about it (strategically, of course).

What Is Cybersecurity ROI?

ROI, at its core, is a measure of how much value you're getting for the money you're spending. In cybersecurity, though, it's less "how much profit did we make?" and more "how much pain did we avoid?"

The Basic Formula:

Cybersecurity ROI = (Value of Risk Avoided – Cost of Security Investment) / Cost of Investment

Sounds simple, right? Well, it's cybersecurity, so buckle up—we're about to dive into assumptions, models, and some light financial acrobatics.

Why ROI Matters in Cybersecurity

- Justifies your budget during planning cycles
- Helps secure executive buy-in for new tools or staff
- Aligns cybersecurity with business goals
- Shows impact in a language CFOs and CEOs understand

TL;DR: If you can't show the value, someone might cut the funding—and leave your digital doors wide open.

Measuring the Value: What Are We Avoiding?

Cyber ROI is often based on what didn't happen thanks to your controls. Sounds abstract, but there are tangible metrics you can use.

1. Cost of a Potential Breach

Use industry averages (e.g., from IBM's "Cost of a Data Breach" report):

- Global avg cost of a breach (2024): ~$4.5M
- Healthcare breaches? Over $10M!

- Small incidents? Still costly (think ransomware at $500K+)

So, if your investment in endpoint protection could prevent one breach, that's massive value.

2. Risk Reduction Percentage

Use risk scoring frameworks (like FAIR or NIST):

- Before investment: 80% likelihood of breach in X area
- After: 30% likelihood
- Multiply that by potential breach impact

Example: Reducing ransomware risk from $1M to $300K saves you $700K.

3. Time and Resource Savings

Tools like SOAR or EDR reduce:

- Analyst workload (fewer false positives)
- Response time
- Downtime during incidents

If a tool saves 100 analyst hours/month, and analysts cost $50/hr, that's $5,000/month in labor value.

Calculating ROI: A Quick Example

Let's say:

- You spend $100K on a new cloud security tool
- You estimate it prevents a breach costing $750K
- You also save $25K in labor/year due to automation

Here's how it stacks up:

ROI = ($750K + $25K - $100K) / $100K = 675% ROI

Yes, really. Security isn't just risk avoidance—it can be a value engine.

Intangible (But Still Valuable) ROI

Some things don't fit neatly into an Excel sheet but still matter to the business.

- Regulatory compliance (avoids fines & lawsuits)
- Customer trust (brand value is hard to regain once lost)
- Investor confidence (especially if you're public)

- Competitive edge (security is a differentiator now)

Want proof? Try doing business in the EU without being GDPR compliant.

Communicating ROI to Stakeholders

It's not just about numbers—it's about telling the story of why security matters, in business terms.

Talk Like This:

- *"This tool reduces breach risk by 60%, saving us $1M in potential losses."*
- *"We improved our phishing resilience by 40%, cutting incident handling time in half."*
- *"With this investment, we met all PCI-DSS controls ahead of audit."*

Avoid:

"We upgraded to AES-256 with hybrid key rotation." (They've already stopped listening.)

Tools and Models to Help You

FAIR Model (Factor Analysis of Information Risk): Great for quantifying risk in financial terms

- **NIST CSF + Risk Tiers:** Useful for maturity progression
- **Cost of a Data Breach Report (IBM):** Free benchmarking data
- **Excel/Power BI dashboards:** Build visual ROI models
- **Gartner TCO/ROI Tools:** Many vendors include calculators to justify their own stuff (just verify assumptions!)

Dealing with the "But We've Never Been Breached" Argument

Ah, the cybersecurity equivalent of "I don't need car insurance—I haven't crashed yet."

Here's what to say:

- *"We haven't been breached because of the investments we've made."*
- *"Our risk profile changes constantly—today's safety doesn't guarantee tomorrow's."*
- *"Would you cancel health insurance because you haven't been sick recently?"*

Sometimes you've got to hit 'em with a real-world case study (like Colonial Pipeline, Equifax, or your industry-specific horror story).

Making ROI Part of Your Cyber Strategy

- Include ROI in every proposal, from firewalls to phishing training

- Tie each investment to a specific business risk or compliance gap
- Track metrics before and after implementation
- Report quarterly ROI snapshots to execs

Eventually, you'll change the narrative from "do we have to spend this?" to "what's our return on this?"

Final Thoughts: Cybersecurity as a Profit Protector

"If your business runs on digital, cybersecurity isn't a cost—it's an investment in survival. And growth. And not going viral for the wrong reasons."

When you speak in terms of ROI, you empower decision-makers to understand the value of cybersecurity—not just fear the consequences of not having it.

And hey, if your ROI story is strong enough, maybe next year they'll finally approve that Red Team budget. Or at least buy you a second monitor.

9.5 Cyber Risk Quantification and Insurance

"Cyber insurance: because sometimes your firewall isn't enough... and neither is a bucket of coffee when things go sideways."

We've all been there: some exec strolls into the war room after hearing about the latest mega-breach and says, "So... we're covered by cyber insurance, right?"

Cue the awkward silence.

Cyber insurance isn't some magical "get out of jail free" card. It's a tool—one piece of your cyber risk strategy—and to use it effectively, you need to quantify your cyber risk first. You know, put numbers to the madness.

So let's get into how you measure cyber risk like a boss—and then use that info to actually make smart decisions (like how much coverage you really need and what fine print to avoid like malware in an email attachment).

What Is Cyber Risk Quantification?

Cyber Risk Quantification (CRQ) is the art (and science) of answering this question:

"If a cyber event happens, how bad could it be—and what are the chances it'll happen?"

It turns security risk into financial terms executives and insurers understand.

Why does this matter? Because:

- It gets you better funding
- It improves decision-making
- It keeps insurance premiums realistic
- It prevents "uh-oh" moments when your claim gets denied

Quantifying Risk: Turning Fear into Math

The two big components of cyber risk quantification are:

1. Impact

What's the cost if the bad thing happens?

- Lost revenue from downtime
- Cost of forensic investigations
- Legal fees and fines
- Customer churn (hello, brand damage)

- Data recovery and ransomware payments

Rule of thumb: Go deep on your crown jewels—not every risk is created equal.

2. Likelihood

What are the chances of it happening?

- Based on threat intel, historical incidents, vulnerabilities
- Can be high, medium, low... or better yet, percentage probabilities

If your CRM system has weak controls and it's constantly scanned by bots, chances are not in your favor.

Pro Tip: Use This Simple Formula

Risk = Likelihood x Impact

So if a threat has a 40% chance of happening, and it could cost you $2M:

Expected Risk Exposure = 0.4 x $2,000,000 = $800,000

That's a solid number to bring into budget and insurance discussions. It makes you look like a cybersecurity Jedi, and it's hard to argue with math.

Tools and Frameworks That Help

- **FAIR (Factor Analysis of Information Risk):** The industry gold standard for financial cyber risk quantification
- **Monte Carlo Simulations:** For modeling risk outcomes based on a range of possibilities
- **NIST 800-30:** Risk assessment framework with qualitative and semi-quantitative options
- **RiskLens, Kovrr, X-Analytics:** Commercial tools that quantify risk and connect it to business outcomes

Enter Cyber Insurance: Your Last Line of Defense

Cyber insurance is like a parachute—you hope you never need it, but you really want it to work when you do.

Here's what it usually covers:

- Data breach response costs
- Business interruption (lost income during downtime)
- Legal and regulatory fines
- Ransomware payments (though this is increasingly scrutinized)
- PR and brand repair

But like any insurance, the devil's in the exclusions—and there are plenty.

Common Coverage Pitfalls to Watch For

War Exclusions

Some policies won't cover nation-state attacks. Problem is... how do you prove who attacked you?

Negligence Clauses

Didn't patch known vulnerabilities? Didn't enforce MFA? They might deny your claim.

Outdated Risk Assessments

If your risk profile has changed significantly (e.g., moved to the cloud, acquired a company), and you didn't update your policy—uh-oh.

Sub-Limits

You might think you have $5M coverage, but only $500K applies to ransomware. Sneaky.

Talking to Insurers: What They Look For

Insurers are getting smarter. They're not just handing out policies like candy anymore. Expect them to ask:

- Do you have MFA?
- Do you conduct regular risk assessments?
- Are backups tested and segmented?
- Do you have an incident response plan?
- Is endpoint detection deployed?

If you answer "no" to too many of those... they might ghost you. Or worse—quote you a premium that makes your CFO weep.

How to Determine the Right Amount of Coverage

You don't need a magic number—you need an informed one. Use your risk quantification to drive this.

Ask:

- What's the max loss from a major breach?
- What's our current risk appetite?
- What controls reduce our exposure?
- How much risk are we willing to transfer?

Example: If your maximum foreseeable cyber loss is $10M and your controls reduce it to $3M, maybe you insure the remaining $3M—plus a bit more to be safe.

Cyber Risk + Insurance = A Continuous Cycle

Risk changes. So should your insurance.

- Update your assessments quarterly
- Revisit your policy annually
- Engage insurers with real data, not guesstimates
- Coordinate with legal, finance, and IT to keep coverage relevant

Real Talk: Is Cyber Insurance Worth It?

Short answer: Yes—but only if:

- You treat it as a backup, not your primary defense
- You understand what's covered and what's not
- You actively manage your security posture

Think of it like flood insurance: just because you have it doesn't mean you leave the front door open during a hurricane.

Final Thoughts: Quantify It or Lose It

"If you can't measure it, you can't manage it—and you sure as heck can't insure it."

Cyber risk quantification gives you the financial lens to guide everything from board discussions to insurance negotiations. It makes security decisions more strategic and less reactive.

And cyber insurance? It's a critical part of the mix. Not a silver bullet, but a strong safety net—if you've done your homework.

So next time someone says "Do we need cyber insurance?" you'll be ready to respond with risk numbers, probability graphs, and maybe even a few Monte Carlo simulations to spice things up.

Chapter 10: Building a Cyber-Resilient Organization

Cybersecurity isn't just a team—it's the whole company wearing digital armor and refusing to click on shady emails. From the janitor to the CEO, resilience means bouncing back from digital disasters like a ninja wrapped in firewall tape. Cue the inspirational montage music!

This final chapter explores the holistic approach required to embed cybersecurity into an organization's DNA. You'll discover how to build a culture of security awareness, implement regular training, conduct red team exercises, and align security goals with business strategy. Cyber resilience is not about never falling—it's about always getting back up, stronger and smarter.

10.1 Culture of Cybersecurity Awareness

"*They say culture eats strategy for breakfast. In cybersecurity, it also chews through your firewall and clicks every phishing link before lunch.*"

Let's be honest: when you think about cybersecurity, the first thing that comes to mind probably isn't "culture." Maybe it's encryption, maybe it's firewalls, or maybe it's Kevin from IT muttering darkly while rebooting the server for the fourth time today.

But here's the thing—cybersecurity culture is the invisible force that either protects your organization... or invites chaos in through the front door, with a cheery smile and a dangerously weak password.

So what is a cybersecurity culture, and how do we build one that actually works? Glad you asked. Let's dive in—with a little humor, a lot of practicality, and zero judgment (okay, maybe just a little if you're still using "admin" as a username).

What Is a Culture of Cybersecurity Awareness?

A culture of cybersecurity awareness means your people—all your people, from the CEO to the intern—understand the cyber risks around them and take everyday actions to reduce those risks.

It's not about turning everyone into a hacker-busting superhero.

It's about making smart, secure behavior a habit.

Just like wearing a seatbelt or locking your front door.

Why Culture Matters More Than You Think

Because humans are the weakest link. Not because they're lazy or dumb—just because they're... well, human.

- 90% of breaches still start with a phishing email
- People reuse passwords like they reuse coffee cups
- USB sticks are mysteriously irresistible
- "Click here to see a cute cat video" works way too often

You can spend millions on security tech, but if Dave from accounting downloads "free tax software" from a sketchy site... you're toast.

Building Blocks of a Cyber-Aware Culture

1. Leadership Buy-In

It starts at the top. If the execs treat security like a box to tick, so will everyone else.

Get them on board:

- Share real-world cyber horror stories
- Tie awareness to business continuity
- Have them participate in training and campaigns (yes, they have to take the quiz too!)

2. Continuous Education (Not Death by PowerPoint)

Security training doesn't have to be soul-crushing.

Keep it:

- **Bite-sized:** Think micro-lessons, 5–10 mins max
- **Interactive:** Games, quizzes, simulations
- **Relevant:** Tailor it to roles—don't teach the receptionist how to threat hunt (unless she's into it)

Bonus points for humor and memes. Your people are more likely to remember "Phishy McPhishface" than a dry paragraph about email hygiene.

3. Make It Personal

People care more when they see how it affects them:

- Identity theft
- Bank fraud
- Embarrassing leaks of that vacation photo

Teach them how to secure their personal lives—then they'll bring that behavior to work.

What Good Cyber Culture Sounds Like

- "That email looks weird—I'm going to report it."
- "I locked my screen, even though I was just grabbing coffee."
- "Let's use the secure file share instead of emailing this Excel sheet with all our customer data."

Now contrast that with:

- *"It's fine, we've never been hacked before."*
- *"This password is easy to remember—'12345678.'"*
- *"Ugh, another security update? Skip."*

Embedding Awareness into the Daily Grind

Security shouldn't feel like a special event. It should be part of how work gets done.

Here's how:

- Add security checks into onboarding
- Include phishing tests regularly (but don't shame people)
- Put posters near coffee machines (because caffeine = learning)
- Use Slack/Teams channels for weekly tips or "threat of the week" alerts

And don't forget to celebrate security wins. Did someone report a phishing email? High five, maybe even a gift card!

The Power of Peer Pressure (In a Good Way)

Security becomes real when coworkers hold each other accountable.

- *"Hey, don't plug in random USBs."*
- *"We should really use MFA for that tool."*
- *"Let's password-protect that file before sending it."*

It's not about tattling—it's about looking out for one another. Like a cyber neighborhood watch.

Common Culture Killers (And How to Avoid Them)

Culture Killer	What It Looks Like	Fix It With
Fear-Based Messaging	"One click and we all die!"	Positive reinforcement and empathy
Inconsistent Leadership	"Rules for thee, not for me"	Exec participation and transparency
Training Overload	"Here's your 90-minute annual training..."	Microlearning and frequent nudges
Lack of Feedback Loops	No idea what works or doesn't	Surveys, engagement tracking, performance reviews

Remember: you can't scare people into caring. But you can inspire them to be part of the solution.

Metrics That Matter

You can't improve what you don't measure. Track:

- Phishing reporting rates
- Click rates on fake phishing tests
- Completion of training programs
- Security incident trends over time

- Employee feedback on training

If your training isn't changing behavior, it's time to rethink the approach.

Wrapping It Up (With a Big, Secure Bow)

"A strong cybersecurity culture doesn't mean your team never makes mistakes—it means they know how to recognize, report, and respond when they do."

Security isn't just a technical problem. It's a human problem with human solutions. You don't need an army of experts—you need a team of aware, engaged, and slightly paranoid employees who know that they are the first line of defense.

So go forth. Train. Meme. Celebrate small wins. And if all else fails, just make the training about cat videos and coffee.

10.2 Security Training and Continuous Education

"You wouldn't give someone a car without teaching them to drive... so why hand out laptops without some cyber survival training?"

Imagine if pilots only trained once at the start of their careers and never again. Terrifying, right? Well, in cybersecurity, a lot of organizations are basically doing that—but with sensitive data, client trust, and millions in risk on the line.

Welcome to the wild world of security training and continuous education, where the biggest risk isn't just a hacker... it's complacency.

Let's break down how to turn your workforce into a human firewall that evolves with the threats—not just one that checks a box once a year and forgets everything by lunchtime.

Why Annual Security Training Is (Probably) Useless

Okay, maybe not completely useless—but if your company's training strategy is just one dry, annual PowerPoint presentation followed by a quiz with questions like:

"Is it OK to write your password on a sticky note? A) Yes B) No C) Maybe"

...then Houston, we have a problem.

Modern threats evolve constantly, and so should your people's awareness and knowledge.

Cybersecurity education must be:

- Continuous
- Engaging
- Relevant
- Role-specific

Or else it's just... noise. ◈

Pillars of an Effective Training Program

1. Continuous Learning

Security is not a "set it and forget it" thing. Neither is training.

Here's what ongoing training looks like:

- Monthly micro-lessons
- Real-world scenario drills

- Gamified learning modules
- News-based awareness updates ("Here's how that recent breach happened...")

People remember what's repeated and reinforced. Just like your favorite catchy (and mildly annoying) pop song.

2. Role-Based Training

Don't make everyone learn about firewall configs (unless they're into that sort of thing). Customize training based on:

- **Department** (finance, HR, dev, legal)
- **Access level** (admin vs user)
- **Risk exposure** (remote employees, execs, third-party contractors)
- HR learns about phishing and data privacy.
- Developers learn about secure coding practices.
- Execs learn how to read cyber risk dashboards (and not just nod thoughtfully).

3. Make It Fun (Or At Least Not Soul-Crushing)

Training doesn't have to be a drag. Seriously.

Mix it up:

- Interactive phishing simulations
- Escape room-style cyber games
- Quizzes with prizes
- Memes and comic strips for reinforcement
- Leaderboards (yes, competition works!)

The goal? Create positive engagement.

The moment people start rolling their eyes at your security emails—you've already lost them.

4. Test and Reinforce Behavior

Here's the kicker: knowing ≠ doing.

So don't just train... test.

Run:

- Surprise phishing tests

- USB drop experiments (label one "employee salary spreadsheet" and see who bites)
- Incident response drills
- Password strength audits

Then follow up with feedback—not finger-pointing. This is about growth, not shame.

Training for Everyone: From Interns to the C-Suite

Audience	What They Need to Know
Interns	Phishing basics, safe browsing, password hygiene
Employees	Role-based threats, reporting procedures
IT/Developers	Secure coding, patching, monitoring
Executives	Risk management, reputation protection, governance
Board Members	Strategic impact, investment prioritization

Everyone's got skin in the game. Don't assume "smart people" automatically understand cybersecurity. Smart people also fall for deepfakes and scam calls.

Feedback Loops & Program Improvement

Want your training to actually improve over time? Ask questions like:

- Did people enjoy the training?
- What stuck with them?
- What didn't land?
- What behavior changed?

Use surveys, participation data, and test results to evolve your program like a digital Pokémon.

And yes, it's okay to pivot. What worked last year might feel outdated this year (looking at you, "Cyber Hygiene 101" slide deck from 2018).

Pro Tips for Cybersecurity Training Wins

- Make it part of onboarding
- Tie it to real-world events ("Here's how someone got hacked on LinkedIn last week...")
- Reward good behavior (gift cards, kudos, digital badges)
- Create internal champions—security advocates within teams

- Keep communication lines open—"Report, don't fear" should be the motto

People need to feel safe to ask dumb questions, report near misses, and admit mistakes. That's how you build a truly resilient culture.

But What About Training Fatigue?

Fair question. Yes, people will get tired if training feels:

- Irrelevant
- Repetitive
- Punitive
- Pointless

Combat this by:

- Rotating content styles
- Focusing on why not just what
- Giving people a voice in the content (e.g., "What cyber topics confuse you most?")

And most importantly... don't treat training as punishment. If someone fails a phishing test, that's an opportunity—not a reason to drag them into the cyber equivalent of detention.

Final Thoughts: Education Is Defense

"In the game of cyber, knowledge isn't just power—it's armor."

Tech can fail. Firewalls can falter. But a well-trained, aware team? That's the kind of protection money can't buy (though, yes, you should budget for training).

Your best defense isn't in the data center—it's walking around your office (or sitting on Zoom with their camera off, let's be real). Give them the tools to defend themselves—and your organization will be safer for it.

10.3 Red Team vs Blue Team Exercises

"Welcome to the ultimate office showdown: Red Team vs Blue Team — where breaking stuff is encouraged, defending your turf is mandatory, and nobody gets fired (hopefully)."

Alright, picture this: your IT team is calmly sipping their fourth coffee of the day, when suddenly... BAM! Simulated ransomware attack. Your systems are going haywire. An email from "CEO@DefinitelyNotFake.com" demands Bitcoin. The printer starts spitting out ASCII skulls.

No, it's not the beginning of a weird tech horror movie—it's a Red Team vs Blue Team exercise, baby. And it's one of the most fun, chaotic, and valuable tools in your cybersecurity playbook.

If you've ever wanted to turn your cyber defense team into a group of elite digital ninjas or unleash your inner hacker (ethically, of course), keep reading.

What Are Red Team vs Blue Team Exercises?

Think of it like cybersecurity capture-the-flag, but with real consequences and much less outdoor activity.

- **Red Team** = The attackers. Their job? Simulate how real-world hackers would try to break into your systems. Think phishing, exploiting vulnerabilities, social engineering, and general mischief.

- **Blue Team** = The defenders. Their mission? Detect, respond, and shut it down before anything goes boom.

The goal? To stress test your security controls, policies, and people—in real time, under pressure.

And yes, it can get intense. In the best way.

Why These Exercises Matter

Cybersecurity isn't about "if" anymore—it's about when. Red vs Blue simulations give you:

- A live-fire environment to test your defenses

- Real insight into detection and response gaps

- A better understanding of how your people react to chaos

- A sandbox for learning without actual business impact (unless your fake CEO accidentally gets a real ransomware email... whoops)

It's the difference between reading about a fire drill and actually running down 10 flights of stairs with your shoelaces untied.

Red Team 101: The Ethical Offense

Red Teams are made up of penetration testers, social engineers, or anyone with a dark hoodie and a legal agreement not to wreck your network.

Their weapons of choice:

- Phishing campaigns
- Exploit toolkits (e.g. Metasploit, Cobalt Strike)
- Physical intrusion (yes, they'll try to sneak into your building)
- Credential harvesting
- Malware simulations

Their mindset: "How would a real attacker break this?"

And believe me—they're very creative. If there's a crack in the wall, they'll widen it. If there's no crack, they'll make one.

Blue Team 101: The Cyber Defenders

Blue Teams are the guardians of the galaxy (or at least your Active Directory).

Their tools:

- SIEMs and EDRs (like Splunk, SentinelOne, etc.)
- Incident response playbooks
- Firewall rules and monitoring dashboards
- Log analysis
- Network segmentation and access control

Their goal? Detect the attack early, mitigate the damage, kick the Red Team out, and laugh in victory while high-fiving in slow motion.

(Okay, maybe not the last part. But still.)

How a Typical Exercise Goes Down

Here's a simplified flow:

Planning Phase

- Define scope and rules (e.g. "Don't touch production payroll.")
- Pick the teams (Red, Blue, sometimes Purple — more on that later)
- Align with execs and make sure Legal is aware

Execution Phase

- Red Team launches their attacks
- Blue Team monitors, detects, and responds
- Chaos ensues... hopefully, in a controlled and educational way

Debrief Phase

- Post-mortem: What worked? What failed? Who clicked what?
- Lessons learned and improvement planning
- Document everything (bonus points if you use memes in the report)

Enter the Purple Team

No, it's not a Prince tribute band (though that would be cool).

The Purple Team bridges the gap between Red and Blue—working collaboratively instead of competitively.

- They observe both sides
- Share insights in real-time
- Help teams learn from each other

Think of them as the cyber referees... or marriage counselors for your offense and defense.

Making It Real: Customizing for Your Org

You don't need a six-figure budget or a cyber warfare trailer to run these.

Start small:

- Simulate a phishing attack on one department
- Test your incident response to a suspicious login from overseas
- Use tabletop exercises for low-budget scenario walkthroughs (still very effective!)

As you grow:

- Try full-scale multi-day simulations
- Add in physical security tests (e.g., can someone tailgate into the office?)
- Involve execs to see how they'd respond to breach notifications

Pro tip: name your Red Team ops with dramatic code names. "Operation Ghost Panda" sounds way cooler than "Phishing Test 3."

Pitfalls to Avoid

Let's not blow up your network in the name of learning, okay?

- Don't test in production without strict guardrails
- Don't embarrass employees—this is not "gotcha" training
- Don't forget documentation (no one likes the post-game amnesia)

And most importantly: don't forget recovery. Your Blue Team needs time to reset and de-stress, especially after a hectic simulation.

Give them donuts. They earned it.

What You Should Track

- Time to detection (how long until Blue saw the attack?)
- Time to containment and recovery
- Number of people who fell for social engineering
- Logging gaps (what did your tools miss?)
- Policy breakdowns (did anyone ignore the response plan?)

These metrics are pure gold for improving your cyber posture.

Wrapping Up: Cyber Kung Fu for the Whole Team

"Red Team vs Blue Team isn't about winning or losing—it's about learning to fight smarter next time."

These exercises build muscle memory. They reveal blind spots. And honestly? They bring a little bit of adrenaline-fueled excitement to the sometimes-boring world of policies and protocols.

Whether your Red Team is made of elite pen-testers or Steve from IT in a hoodie and a mischievous grin—this practice works. Run it often. Debrief honestly. Improve continuously.

And hey—next time someone asks, "How prepared are we for an attack?"

You'll be able to smile and say:

"Oh, we've already been attacked. And we kicked their simulated butt."

10.4 Integrating Cybersecurity into Business Strategy

"*If cybersecurity isn't at the business table, it's probably being served for lunch.*"

Let's be honest: for far too long, cybersecurity has been treated like the office smoke detector—important, but mostly ignored unless something's literally on fire.

But in today's hyper-digital, reputation-on-the-line, compliance-minefield kind of world, that just won't cut it. Cybersecurity isn't just an IT issue anymore—it's a strategic business enabler. Yep, I said it. A business enabler.

When cybersecurity is embedded into your business strategy from day one—not bolted on as an afterthought—it becomes a competitive advantage, not just a cost center.

Let's break down how we make that happen... and how to stop security from being the corporate party pooper.

Why Should Cybersecurity Be in the Boardroom?

Imagine launching a new mobile app... without asking legal about compliance. Risky, right?

Now imagine doing it without involving cybersecurity. That's not just risky—it's potentially disastrous.

Cyber threats don't just hit your servers—they hit:

- Customer trust
- Investor confidence
- Brand reputation
- Operational continuity
- Share price (yep, that too)

Basically, everything the board does care about.

So, if cybersecurity isn't part of business decision-making at the top, you're driving without brakes and hoping for the best.

The Cyber-Strategy Feedback Loop

To integrate cybersecurity effectively, you need a two-way street between security and business goals.

Here's the loop:

Understand the Business Strategy

- What are the revenue streams?
- What digital assets are critical?

- Are you expanding into new markets, launching products, merging?

Identify the Cyber Impacts

- How do threats affect those goals?
- Where are the vulnerabilities tied to business functions?

Adjust Security Priorities Accordingly

- Tailor risk management to protect high-value assets
- Allocate security resources where they matter most

Inform Strategy with Cyber Insights

- Help leadership see new risks AND opportunities through a cyber lens

Rinse. Repeat. Grow stronger.

Security as a Strategic Business Partner (Not the Department of "No")

Here's a truth bomb: Security teams have a bit of a PR problem.

They're often seen as blockers:

- *"No, you can't launch that product without 57 approvals."*
- *"No, that tool isn't secure."*
- *"No, no, no."*

But we need to flip the script.

Great cybersecurity teams say:

"Yes, and here's how we do it securely."

They enable innovation, accelerate go-to-market timelines, and ensure customer data doesn't end up trending on Reddit.

Cyber Risk = Business Risk

You know what really gets execs and investors listening? Numbers. Dollar signs. Impact.

Instead of saying:

"There's a vulnerability in our S3 bucket."

Say:

"This issue could lead to a $2M regulatory fine and a 14% drop in customer retention if exploited."

That, my friend, is how you speak fluent business.

Leverage risk quantification (like FAIR) to translate cyber risk into:

- Financial exposure
- Legal consequences
- Operational downtime
- Strategic delays

Speak their language, and suddenly you're not just the tech guy—you're the trusted advisor.

Key Ways to Embed Security Into Strategy

Here's your battle plan for actually integrating cybersecurity into the business machine:

1. Involve Security Early in Projects

Security should be at the table during:

- Product design
- Vendor selection
- Digital transformation
- M&A discussions
- Cloud migrations

Waiting until after launch? That's like installing seatbelts after the crash.

2. Align Security KPIs with Business KPIs

If your company goal is to "increase customer adoption by 40%," your cyber goal might be "reduce user friction in MFA while maintaining secure access."

Security must align with outcomes—not just audit checklists.

3. Make Risk-Based Decisions

Not all risks are created equal. A threat to your mobile app's user data ≠ someone clicking a spam link on the intern's PC (sorry, interns).

Use a risk-based approach to prioritize what matters, and let low-risk issues simmer on the back burner (with supervision).

4. Build Cyber Into Strategic Planning Cycles

- **Annual planning?** Include cyber roadmap.

- **Budgeting process?** Fund security initiatives based on risk and value.
- **New market entry?** Evaluate threat landscape and local compliance needs.

Security shouldn't be a reactive emergency budget—it should be part of the financial plan from the get-go.

Case in Point: Cyber as a Competitive Advantage

Companies that do this well don't just survive—they thrive. Some examples:

- **Apple:** Built privacy and security into their brand.
- **Salesforce:** Turned transparency into trust with real-time trust dashboards.
- **Banks:** Market "security-first" platforms as a feature, not a footnote.

By making security part of your value prop, you build customer loyalty, partner trust, and even market differentiation.

What Happens When You Don't

Now, let's flip the coin.

Ignoring cybersecurity as a strategic priority leads to:

- Breaches that derail product launches
- Lawsuits and compliance fines
- Executive resignations
- Stock drops
- Long-term brand erosion

A single breach can undo years of brand building. Just ask any company that's made headlines for the wrong reasons.

Final Thoughts: Strategy Without Security Is Just Guesswork

"If you don't plan for cyber risks, you're not making a business strategy—you're making a wish list."

Embedding cybersecurity into business strategy isn't just smart—it's necessary.

- It protects what matters.
- It fuels confident innovation.
- It builds trust with customers and regulators.

And—let's not forget—it helps you sleep better at night.

So, bring your security leaders into strategic conversations. Encourage them to learn the business. And empower them to say "yes"—securely.

Because in the long run, integrating cybersecurity isn't about fear. It's about resilience, reputation, and ROI.

10.5 Leadership in Cyber Risk Management

"In the world of cyber risk, leadership isn't about having all the answers. It's about being the calmest person in the room when everything's on fire —digitally, of course."

Let's face it—when someone yells "cyberattack!" in the boardroom, people tend to freak out. Eyes widen, panic sets in, and someone inevitably asks, "Did we back up the backups?"

In those moments—and ideally before them—what matters most isn't just firewalls or antivirus software. It's leadership.

Yep, plain old-fashioned, decision-making, tone-setting, responsibility-owning leadership.

And no, it's not just the CISO's job anymore. Cyber risk leadership is a full-contact sport that involves everyone from the CEO to the intern who still clicks "Enable Macros" in Word documents.

So let's talk about what great cyber risk leadership looks like—and how to go from "tech manager" to full-on cyber commander-in-chief.

What Is Cyber Risk Leadership, Really?

Cyber risk leadership means more than just being the loudest person in the room shouting "Zero Trust!" at random intervals.

It means:

- Making security a strategic priority
- Creating a culture of shared responsibility
- Driving accountability across departments
- Empowering your teams to respond quickly and smartly when stuff hits the fan

And most importantly, it means being able to explain cyber risk to non-technical folks without sounding like you're pitching a sci-fi movie.

Traits of an Effective Cyber Risk Leader

You don't need a hoodie, a black belt in Linux, or even a degree in cybersecurity to lead well in this space. What you need is:

1. Vision

Think beyond the next patch cycle. Know where the organization is heading and anticipate what cyber threats might block the path.

Great cyber leaders are part oracle, part realist.

2. Communication Skills

Can you explain ransomware to the board without using acronyms or scaring them into paralysis? Can you talk "risk" instead of "rootkit"?

If yes, you win.

3. Cross-Functional Influence

You can't silo cybersecurity anymore. A real leader brings finance, HR, ops, and marketing into the conversation. (Even if it means showing them a meme-filled deck.)

4. Crisis Management

When the alert lights go red and people start sweating, you're the calm voice saying: "We trained for this. Let's execute."

5. Empathy

Security isn't always easy for non-tech folks. Lead with understanding, not condescension. People remember how you made them feel—not just what you said.

The Cyber Chain of Command

Let's break down who plays what role in the cyber risk leadership hierarchy. (Spoiler: it's not just the IT department.)

CEO / Executive Leadership

- Sets the tone at the top
- Ensures cybersecurity is aligned with business strategy
- Allocates proper funding and support
- Doesn't forward phishing emails "just to see what happens"

CISO (Chief Information Security Officer)

- Translates business objectives into security priorities
- Manages the cyber risk program
- Communicates with the board in business language
- Keeps calm and carries a zero-day response plan

Board of Directors

- Holds leadership accountable for risk
- Oversees security posture as part of governance
- Must be educated on threats, not just quarterly numbers

Department Heads (HR, Finance, Legal, Ops, etc.)

- Own their department's security responsibilities
- Work with cyber leaders to ensure compliance and readiness
- Avoid being "that team" that ignored the MFA rollout

Everyone Else

- Participates in awareness training
- Reports suspicious behavior
- Doesn't write passwords on sticky notes (hopefully)

Speaking the Language of the Board

One of the toughest leadership challenges in cyber is translating geek-speak into boardroom-speak.

Don't say:

"We had an intrusion via a known CVE on our Apache server."

Do say:

"We had a vulnerability in our web system that could have exposed customer data. We caught it early, and here's how we mitigated the risk."

Stick to:

- Business impact
- Financial exposure
- Reputational risk
- Regulatory implications

Skip the part about kernel panic logs unless someone really insists.

Building a Security Culture from the Top Down

Culture eats strategy for breakfast—and your security program is no exception.

Cyber risk leadership means creating a culture where:

- Reporting incidents is encouraged, not punished
- Awareness training is engaging, not just "click-and-forget"
- Employees understand why security matters to the business

Pro tip: get creative. Use humor. Use stories. Use that phishing email about the "free iPhone" as a learning moment—not a beatdown.

Security culture starts with leadership. If you take it seriously (but not stiffly), your people will too.

Practical Steps to Level Up Your Cyber Risk Leadership

Hold Regular Cyber Briefings with Executives

Keep them informed without overwhelming them. Stick to key risks, progress, and what needs escalation.

Create Clear Ownership of Cyber Responsibilities

Everyone should know who does what, especially during incidents.

Invest in Leadership Training for Security Staff

Your best tech experts may not be natural communicators. Train them to lead, not just patch.

Champion Cybersecurity in Strategic Initiatives

Launching a new product? Expanding into new markets? Make sure cyber is in the room before the contracts are signed.

Celebrate Security Wins

Did the team catch a phishing attempt? Roll out a new secure login method? Celebrate it! Positive reinforcement builds momentum.

Fun Leadership Fails (That Actually Happened)

Because what would a leadership chapter be without a little cautionary comic relief?

- A VP once disabled MFA because "it was annoying." They got breached within a week.
- An exec clicked a phishing link, then asked IT to "just delete the virus." That's not how any of this works.
- A CEO used "123456" as a password because "it's easy to remember." Facepalm.

Remember: a chain is only as strong as its least secure exec.

Final Thought: You Don't Have to Be a Hacker to Lead Cyber Risk

"Being a great cyber risk leader isn't about knowing how to write Python exploits—it's about knowing how to protect your people, your data, and your mission."

If you can:

- Communicate clearly
- Make smart decisions under pressure

- Rally a team around a shared goal

Then congratulations—you've got the makings of a strong cyber leader.

Now go forth, secure the kingdom, and try not to accidentally reply-all to the phishing test email again.

So, we made it. You, me, and probably a few hundred digital threats that we've now stared down like cybersecurity cowboys. If you've read this far, congratulations—you are officially risk-aware, slightly more paranoid (in the good way), and equipped with enough cybersecurity knowledge to make your old IT teacher proud and your hacker enemies weep.

This book—**Cyber Security Risk Management Handbook: Fortify, Protect, Defend**—has taken us on a rollercoaster through the digital Wild West. From learning how to identify risks like a digital Sherlock Holmes, to prioritizing them like a stressed-out project manager with only three sticky notes left, we've tackled the full lifecycle of risk management. We explored defense strategies that go beyond just "install antivirus," looked at how to survive an incident without losing our minds (or jobs), and even peeked into the terrifyingly cool future of AI, quantum threats, and WiFi-enabled blenders that might just be spying on us.

But more than that, I hope this book showed you that cybersecurity isn't just for hoodie-wearing hackers and gloomy tech folks muttering acronyms. It's for business owners, IT pros, students, managers, and literally anyone who has ever clicked on an email and thought, "Hmm... that link looks sketchy." (Spoiler: it was.)

Cyber risk management is part art, part science, and part just plain common sense. It's not about being perfect—it's about being prepared. It's not about fearing the threat—it's about outsmarting it. And guess what? You can absolutely do this.

Now, a moment for some honest, heartfelt gratitude.

To you, dear reader—thank you. Thank you for picking up this book, flipping through its pages (or scrolling, if you're the digital kind), and giving your time to learn, laugh, and level up your cyber defense mindset. Whether you're here to protect your company, your data, or just your mom from getting phished again (bless her heart), I appreciate you more than you know. Without readers like you, this book would just be me talking to myself—and I already do enough of that in server rooms at 3 a.m.

I know cybersecurity risk management isn't exactly beach-reading material (unless you're really hardcore), but you showed up. You cared enough to invest in protecting what matters. And that, my friend, puts you way ahead of the curve.

So here's to you: the curious, the cautious, the committed. Keep learning, keep questioning, and never stop fortifying, protecting, and defending. The world needs more cyber heroes like you—armor up, carry on, and don't forget to patch your systems.

And hey... next time something suspicious happens, at least now you'll know exactly which chapter to flip to.

Cheers,

Dravenius Queltharan

(Recovering incident responder, eternal coffee drinker, your cyber risk tour guide)

www.ingramcontent.com/pod-product-compliance
Lightning Source LLC
LaVergne TN
LVHW060033210926
848481LV00013B/3856